Robert Swan

Series Editor: Marian

C000202646

Atone

Ian McEwan

Philip Allan Updates
Market Place
Deddington
Oxfordshire
OX15 0SE

Orders

Bookpoint Ltd, 130 Milton Park, Abingdon, Oxfordshire, OX14 4SB
tel: 01235 827720
fax: 01235 400454
e-mail: uk.orders@bookpoint.co.uk
Lines are open 9.00 a.m.–5.00 p.m., Monday to Saturday, with a 24-hour message
answering service. You can also order through the Philip Allan Updates website:
www.philipallan.co.uk

© Philip Allan Updates 2006

ISBN-13 978-1-84489-605-9
ISBN-10 1-84489-605-6

All rights reserved; no part of this publication may be reproduced, stored in
a retrieval system, or transmitted, in any form or by any means, electronic,
mechanical, photocopying, recording or otherwise without either the prior
written permission of Philip Allan Updates or a licence permitting restricted
copying in the United Kingdom issued by the Copyright Licensing Agency Ltd,
90 Tottenham Court Road, London W1T 4LP.

In all cases we have attempted to trace and credit copyright owners of material used.

Printed by Raithby, Lawrence and Co Ltd, Leicester

Environmental information
The paper on which this title is printed is sourced from mills using wood from
managed, sustainable forests.

Contents

Introduction

Aims of the guide

The purpose of this Student Text Guide to Ian McEwan's best-selling novel *Atonement* is to enable you to organise your thoughts and responses to the novel, to deepen your understanding of key features and aspects, and to help you to address the particular requirements of examination questions in order to obtain the best possible grade. It will also prove useful to those writing a coursework piece on the novel as it provides summaries, lists, analyses and references to help with the content and construction of the assignment.

It is assumed that you have already read and studied the novel under the guidance of a teacher or lecturer. This is a revision guide, not an introduction, although some of its content serves the purpose of providing initial background. It can be read in its entirety, or it can be used as a reference guide to specific and separate aspects of the novel.

The remainder of this Introduction consists of the Assessment Objectives, which summarise the requirements of the various exam boards and their schemes of assessment; revision advice, which gives a suggested programme for using the material in the guide; and guidance on writing examination essays.

The Text Guidance section consists of a series of subsections that examine key aspects of the book, including contexts, chapter summaries and commentary, characters, themes and language. Emboldened terms within this section are glossed in the 'Literary terms and concepts' section on pp. 87–88.

The final section, Questions and Answers, gives brief practical advice on writing essay answers of various types, along with mark schemes, model essay plans and some examples of marked work.

Page references are to the Vintage paperback edition (2002, 2005).

Assessment Objectives

The Assessment Objectives (AOs) for A-level English Literature are common to all boards:

AO1	communicate clearly the knowledge, understanding and insight appropriate to literary study, using appropriate terminology and accurate and coherent written expression
AO2i	respond with knowledge and understanding to literary texts of different types and periods

AO2ii	respond with knowledge and understanding to literary texts of different types and periods, exploring and commenting on relationships and comparisons between literary texts
AO3	show detailed understanding of the ways in which writers' choices of form, structure and language shape meanings
AO4	articulate independent opinions and judgements, informed by different interpretations of literary texts by other readers
AO5i	show understanding of the contexts in which literary texts are written and understood
AO5ii	evaluate the significance of cultural, historical and other contextual influences on literary texts and study

A summary of each Assessment Objective is given below and would be worth memorising:

AO1	clarity of written communication
AO2	informed personal response in relation to time and genre (literary context)
AO3	the creative literary process (context of writing)
AO4	critical and interpretative response (context of reading)
AO5	evaluation of influences (cultural context)

Assessment weighting

It is essential that you pay close attention to the Assessment Objectives, and their weighting, for the board for which you are entered. These are what the examiner will be looking for, and you must address them *directly* and *specifically*, in addition to proving general familiarity with and understanding of the text, and being able to present an argument clearly, relevantly and convincingly.

Remember, the examiners are seeking above all else evidence of an *informed personal response* to the text. A revision guide such as this can help you to understand the text and to form your own opinions, but it cannot replace your own ideas and responses as an individual reader.

Revision advice

For the examined units it is possible that either brief or extensive revision will be necessary because the original study of the text took place some time previously. It is therefore useful to know how to approach revision and which tried and tested methods

are considered the most successful for literature exams at all levels, from GCSE to degree finals. Below is a guide on how not to do it — think of reasons why not in each case.

Don't:
- leave it until the last minute
- assume you remember the text well enough and don't need to revise at all
- spend hours designing a beautiful revision schedule
- revise more than one text at the same time
- think you don't need to revise because it is an open-book exam
- decide in advance what you think the questions will be and revise only for those
- try to memorise particular essay plans
- read texts again randomly and aimlessly
- revise for longer than 2 hours in one sitting
- miss school lessons in order to work alone at home
- try to learn a whole ring-binder's worth of work
- tell yourself that character and plot revision is enough
- imagine that watching the video again is the best way to revise
- rely on a study guide instead of the text

There are no short cuts to effective exam revision; the only way to know a text well, and to know your way around it in an exam, is to have done the necessary studying. If you use the following six-stage method you will not only manage to revisit and reassess all previous work on the text but will be able to distil, organise and retain your knowledge.

(1) Between a month and a fortnight before the exam, depending on your schedule, i.e. a simple list of stages with dates, you will need to read the text again, this time taking stock of all the underlinings and marginal annotations. As you read, collect onto sheets of A4 the essential ideas and quotations. The acts of selecting key material and recording it as notes are natural ways of stimulating thought and aiding memory.

(2) Reread the highlighted areas and marginal annotations in your critical extracts and background handouts, and add anything useful from them to your list of notes and quotations. Then read your previous essays and the teacher's comments again. As you look back through essays written earlier in the course you should have the pleasant sensation of realising that you are now able to write much better on the text than you could before. You will also discover that much of your huge file of notes is redundant or repeated, and that you have changed your mind about some beliefs, so the distillation process is not too daunting. Selecting what is important is the way to crystallise your knowledge and understanding.

(3) During the run-up to the exam you need to make lots of practice essay plans to help you identify any gaps in your knowledge and give you practice in planning

in 5–8 minutes. Past-paper titles for you to plan are provided in this guide, some of which can be done as full timed essays — and marked strictly according to exam criteria — which will show whether length and timing are problematic for you. If you have not seen a copy of a real exam paper before you take your first module, ask to see a past paper so that you are familiar with the layout and rubric. For each text you are studying for the examination you need to know exactly which Assessment Objectives are being tested and where the heaviest weighting falls, as well as whether it is a closed or open-book exam. It would also be helpful if your teacher shared with you the examiners' reports on past papers.

(4) About a week before the exam, reduce your two or three sides of A4 notes to the size of a double-sided postcard of very small, dense writing. Collect a group of key words by once again selecting and condensing, using abbreviations for quotations (first and last word), and character and place names (initials). Choosing and writing out the short quotations will help you to focus on the essential issues, and to recall them quickly in the exam. Make sure that your selection covers the main themes and includes examples of imagery, language, style, comments on character, examples of irony and other significant aspects of the text. Previous class discussion and essay writing will have indicated which quotations are useful for almost any essay title; select those that can serve more than one purpose. In this way, a minimum number of quotations can have maximum application.

(5) You now have in a compact, accessible form all the material for any possible essay title. There are only half a dozen themes relevant to a literary text — though be aware that they may be expressed in a variety of ways — so if you have covered these you should not meet with any unpleasant surprises when you read the exam questions. You don't need to refer to your file of paperwork again, or even to the text. For the few days before the exam you can read through your handy postcard notes whenever and wherever you get the opportunity. Each time you read them, which should only take a few minutes, you are reminding yourself of all the information you will be able to recall in the exam to adapt to the general title or to support an analysis of particular passages.

(6) A fresh, active mind works wonders, and information needs time to settle, so don't try to cram just before the exam. Get a good night's sleep the night before so that you will be able to enter the exam room feeling the confidence of the well-prepared candidate.

Writing examination essays

Essay content

One of the key skills you are being asked to demonstrate at A-level is the ability to select and tailor your knowledge of the text and its background to the question set in the

exam paper. In order to reach the highest levels, you need to avoid 'pre-packaged' essays that lack focus, relevance and coherence, and that simply contain everything you know about the text. Be ruthless in rejecting irrelevant material, after considering whether it can be made relevant by a change of emphasis. Aim to cover the whole question, not just part of it; your response needs to demonstrate breadth and depth, covering the full range of text elements: character, event, theme and language. Essay questions are likely to refer to the key themes of the text, and therefore preparation of the text should involve extensive discussion and practice at manipulating these core themes. An apparently new angle is more likely to be something familiar presented in an unfamiliar way and you should not panic or reject the choice of question because you think you know nothing about it.

Read essay questions twice — the focus is not always immediately obvious. Many of them are several lines long, with several parts or sentences, some of which may be quotations from critics or from the text. You need to be sure of what a title means, and the assumptions behind it, before deciding whether to reject or attempt it.

Different views

Exam titles are open-ended in the sense that there is no obvious right answer, and you would therefore be unwise to give a dismissive, extreme or entirely one-sided response; the question would not have been set if the answer were not debatable. An ability and willingness to see both sides is an Assessment Objective and shows independence of judgement as a reader. Don't be afraid to explore the issues and avoid trying to tie the text into one neat interpretation. If there is ambiguity it is likely to be deliberate on the part of the author and must be discussed; literary texts are complex and often paradoxical, and it would be a misreading of them to suggest that there is only one possible interpretation. You are not expected, however, to argue equally strongly or extensively for both sides of an argument, since personal opinion is an important factor. It is advisable to deal with the alternative view at the beginning of your response, and then construct your own view as the main part of the essay. This makes it less likely that you will appear to cancel out your own line of argument.

Although the essay question may ask you to base your answer on one passage, you should ensure that you also refer to other parts of the text. As long as you stay focused on your main selection of material and on the key words in the question, you will get credit for making brief comments on other supporting material, which could include reference to critical works, works by other authors, or other works by the same author, as well as links to elsewhere in the same text.

Levels of response

A text can be responded to on four levels, but only the fourth one can receive the highest marks.

If you just give a character sketch or account of an incident this is the lowest and purely *descriptive* level, giving evidence of no skill other than being aware of the plot and characters; this does not even require a reading of the text itself. You are dealing only with the question 'What?' and in a limited context.

The next level, at about grade D, is a wider or more detailed *commentary* on events or characters, even making connections between them; but it still does not show real understanding of the text or an ability to interpret its themes.

For a C or low B grade you need to link different areas of the text, enter into *discussion* and explore major issues, though they may be in isolation from each other. This type of response addresses the question 'Why?'

A high B or A grade requires you to perform at an *analytical* level, showing an ability to think conceptually and to range across the whole text. You need to infer and draw conclusions based on an overview gained through a grasp of the overall themes that provide the coherent framework for the text. As well as character, plot and theme analysis, you will need to discuss language, style and structural elements, and link everything together. The question 'How?' is fully addressed at this level.

Length and timing

You will probably know by now whether length or timing is a problem for you. Although quality matters more than quantity, it is unlikely that you will have been able to fully explore and give a comprehensive answer to the question in fewer than three sides of A4 writing. You will typically have only 1 hour — minus planning and checking time — to write your essay, so you must practise the planning and writing stages under timed conditions until you are confident that you can give a full answer, ideally four sides, within the time limit. Finishing too early is not desirable, since the essay is unlikely to be as good as it could have been if the time had been fully utilised. The secret of length/timing success is to have developed a concise style and a brisk pace so that a lot of material is covered in a short space.

Choosing the right question

If there is a choice, the first skill you must show when presented with the exam paper is the ability to select the questions on your text that are best for you. This is not to say you should always go for the same type of essay, and if the question is not one with which you feel happy for any reason, you should consider the alternative, even if it is not a type you normally prefer. It is unlikely, but possible, that a question will contain a word you are not familiar with, in which case it would be safer to choose the other option.

Do not be tempted to choose a question because of its similarity to one you have already answered. Thinking on the spot usually produces a better result than attempting to recall a previous essay, which may have received only a mediocre mark

in the first place. The exam question is unlikely to have exactly the same focus and your response may seem 'off centre' as a result, as well as stale and perfunctory in expression.

Underlining key words

When you have chosen your question, underline the key words in the title. There may be only one or as many as five or six, and it is essential that you discover how many aspects your response has to cover and fix in your mind the focus the answer must have. An essay that answers only half of the question cannot score top marks, however well that half is executed, and you need to demonstrate your responsiveness to all of the implications of the question. The key words often provide the sub-headings for planning and can suggest the overall approach to the essay.

Planning and structuring

To be convincing, your essay must demonstrate a logical order of thought and a sense of progression towards a conclusion. If you reproduce your ideas in random order as they occur to you, they are unlikely to form a coherent whole. Jumping between unrelated ideas is confusing for the reader and weakens the argument. If you find yourself repeating a quotation or writing 'as I said earlier' or 'as will be discussed later', you have probably not structured your essay effectively. There is no right structure for an essay, as long as there is one.

When planning an essay — which you can afford to spend 7–8 minutes on — you should first brainstorm all the appropriate ideas and material you can think of, making a list in note form and using abbreviations to save time. You should aim for 10–12 separate points — about half a page — which will become the 10 or 12 paragraphs of your essay. If after a few minutes you do not have enough material, quickly switch to the other essay title. Beside each point, in a parallel column, indicate how you will support it. Next, group together the ideas that seem to belong together, and sort them into a logical order, using numbers. Identify which point will be the basis of your conclusion — the one with the overview — and move it to the end. The first points will follow from the essay title and definition of key words, and will be a springboard for your line of argument.

Remember that characters, events and aspects of language exist as vehicles for a text's themes — the real reason why texts are written. You need to become accustomed to planning by theme, using the other three elements to provide support and examples. Material relating to social and historical context needs to be integrated into your response and not just tacked on to the beginning or end.

Your plan should be cancelled with one diagonal line when you have finished writing your essay. The examiner does not want to start reading it by mistake, but will note that it exists, and it will raise expectations of a good essay. Your plan can be flexible — you can add extra material or decide to delete some during the writing stage — but it provides your basic structure and safety net.

Evidence

When selecting a point, check that you can support it adequately and convincingly; if not, substitute a better point. Unsupported assertion does not get much credit in exam essays and gives the impression of desperation or lack of familiarity with the text. Using about three paragraphs to a page, you should structure each paragraph by making a point and then supporting it with textual evidence, and a brief analysis of what it contributes to the overall answer to the question; without proof, paragraphs will be undeveloped and insubstantial.

Support for your argument can take three forms: reference, example or quotation. Aim for a mixture of these forms, as well as of different kinds of evidence (character, plot, image etc.). Quotation is not a substitute for thought or argument; it should support your interpretation and relate directly to the point you are making. It is the most effective way of proving familiarity and confidence in the use of the text, and of validating your claims.

When using other people's ideas as support, you must give credit where it is due, rather than trying to pass them off as your own. It is much more scholarly to attribute the reference, unless it is something which has been completely absorbed into your own interpretation and expressed in your own words. Otherwise, you can acknowledge source material by paraphrasing or summarising it, or by quoting exactly in inverted commas, mentioning the author in each case. A third option, if you have a quotation or idea you want to include but can't remember exactly where it came from, is to say 'as has been claimed by a critic' or 'it has been pointed out that …'.

Choose exactly the right quotation for what you are trying to prove, and use only the words that are appropriate. You can show that you have removed words from a quotation by using the ellipsis symbol (…) to replace the missing section. The cardinal rule is to quote accurately. If in doubt, it is safer to paraphrase than to guess wrongly.

Don't be afraid of using too much quotation; up to a quarter of an essay, or one per sentences, is acceptable. However, quotation for the sake of it, without interpretation or relevance, is useless, and you should aim for short integrated quotations of two or three words rather than longer ones, which take time and space. Short quotations (less than one line of printed text) can be incorporated into your own sentences; longer quotations need to be introduced by a colon, started on a new line, and inset from both margins. If you are considering using such a lengthy quotation, pause and ask yourself if it is all necessary.

If you can't think of the right quotation to prove a point, reconsider whether the point is valid or worth making, or use an example or illustration instead. Remember that a quotation may prove more than one point; rather than repeating it, which weakens its effect, use it as a 'sandwich' between the two ideas it illustrates, which gives the impression of clever planning and structuring.

When making quotations, you do not need to give page references. Never give references instead of the quotation.

Put quotations in inverted commas; underline or use inverted commas for the title of the text.

Openings

Openings are the first indication to the examiner of whether you are an excellent, a mediocre or a weak student; it will be difficult to correct that first impression. By the end of the first paragraph you will have revealed whether you have the ability to write relevantly, accurately and clearly. For the most part, the best way into a literature essay is to define the implications and complexities of the title, starting with the underlined key words, especially if they are abstract concepts with a variety of possible interpretations (such as 'successful' and 'true'). Next, the widest and broadest application of the terms to the text will produce a range of ideas that could themselves be the structural headings for the essay.

As well as indicating the scope and framework for the answer, the introduction should provide brief and relevant contextual information. This may refer to the genre, the setting, the themes or the characters. It should not, however, be any of the following: a full plot synopsis; a summary of the life and work of the author; a repeat of the question; a vague and unfocused comment on life in general; or a list of any kind. Only points directly relevant to the question can be credited, so get started on the analysis as soon as possible. An introduction does not need to be more than a sentence or short paragraph and should never be longer than half a page.

Writing

With a useful plan you can write continuously — without needing to stop and think what to say next — and with fluency and coherence. You will need to write quickly and legibly. Think about appropriate expression and accuracy, asking yourself always 'What exactly am I trying to say?' Try to sound engaged and enthusiastic in your response; examiners are human and are affected by tone as much as the reader is with a text. It is actually possible to enjoy writing an essay, even in exam conditions. Learn and apply the mnemonic acronym ACRID (accurate, concise, relevant, interesting and detailed).

Each paragraph should follow logically from the one before, either to continue the argument or to change its direction. Adverbial paragraph links — such as 'Furthermore', 'However', 'On the other hand' — are vital pointers to the progression of the argument. Paragraphs are a necessary courtesy to the reader and an indicator of point/topic change; paragraphs that are too long or too short reveal repetitive expression and lack of structure, or undeveloped ideas and lack of support respectively.

Avoid tentative or dogmatic statements, which make you sound either vague and uncertain or pompous and arrogant. Don't overstate or become sensational or

emotional; steer clear of cliché and 'waffle'. Use accepted literary conventions, such as discussing literature in the present tense, avoiding calling a reader 'he', and using the surnames only of authors. It is safer to stick to the text itself than speculate about the author's intentions or personal viewpoint. Examiners are not looking for evidence of what you know about the author; they want to see your response to the text, and how you can apply your analysis to the question.

Write in a suitably formal, objective and impersonal style, avoiding ambiguous, repetitive and vague phrases. The aim is always clarity of thought and expression. Use appropriate technical terms to show competence instead of using unnecessary words. It is important to use exactly the right word and not the rough approximation which first comes to mind. Remember that every word should work for you and don't waste time on 'filler' expressions (such as 'As far as the novel is concerned') and adverbial intensifiers (such as 'very' and 'indeed'). Say something once, explore it, prove it and move on; you can only get credit for a point once. You don't need to preface every point with 'I think that' or 'I believe', since the whole essay is supposed to consist of what you think and believe. Don't keep repeating the terms of the title; the whole essay is supposed to be linked to the title, so you don't need to keep saying so. It must always be clear, however, how your point relates to the title, not left to the reader to guess or mind-read what you think the connection may be.

Don't speculate, hypothesise, exaggerate or ask questions — it's your job to answer them. Feelings are not a substitute for thought in an academic essay; 'I feel' is usually a prelude to some unsubstantiated 'gushing'. Don't patronise the author by praising him or her for being clever or achieving something, and avoid copying your teacher through your marginal notes. The examiner will quickly spot if the whole class is using the same phrases, and will then know it is not your own idea that is being expressed. To quote from examiners' comments, to achieve a grade A, candidates are required to 'show a freshness of personal response as opposed to mere repetition of someone else's critical opinions, however good'. Whether the examiner agrees with you or not is irrelevant; it's the quality of the argument that counts.

While you are writing, keep an eye on the clock and aim to finish 5 minutes before the end of the exam to give you checking time. If you find you are running short of time, telescope the argument but try to cover all your points; as an emergency measure, break into notes to show what you would have written. This is better than spending your last precious 5 minutes finishing a particular sentence and not indicating what would have come next if you hadn't miscalculated the time.

Endings

Many students have trouble with endings, which are as important as openings. They are what the whole essay has been working towards and what the examiner has in mind when deciding upon a final mark. An ending needs to be conclusive,

impressive and climactic, and not give the impression that the student has run out of time, ideas or ink. An ineffective ending is often the result of poor planning. Just repeating a point already made or lamely ending with a summary of the essay is a weak way of finishing, and cannot earn any extra marks.

Once again there are techniques for constructing conclusions. You need to take a step back from the close focus of the essay and make a comment that pulls together everything you've been saying and ties it into the overall significance of the text. A quotation from within or outside the text, possibly by the author, can be effective and definitive. You can also refer back to the title, or your opening statement, so that there is a satisfying sense of circularity for the reader, giving the impression that there is no more to be said on this subject.

Checking

Writing fast always causes slips of the mind and pen; these missing letters and words, misnamings of characters and genre confusions, are indistinguishable from ignorance and therefore must be corrected before submission. In addition, unchecked work will give a negative impression of your standards as a literature student, and examiners can always tell when work has been left unchecked.

Allow 5 minutes for checking your essay. Having spent several months studying a text it is worth making sure that your only exam essay on it is as good as you can possibly make it. A few minutes spent checking can make the difference of a grade. Don't be afraid to cross words or phrases out; neat writing and immaculate pres-entation are not skills being assessed, but 'accurate and coherent written expression' is. As long as it is done neatly with one line, and the replacement word is written above legibly, correction counts in your favour rather than against you. Insert an asterisk in the text and put a longer addition at the bottom of the essay rather than trying to cram it into the margin, where it will be difficult to read and is encroaching on examiner territory. If you have forgotten to change paragraphs often enough, put in markers (//) when checking to show where a paragraph indentation should be.

When you check, you are no longer the writer but the reader of the text you have created, and a stranger too. Can you follow its line of argument? Are the facts accurate? Does it hang together? Is the vocabulary explicit? Is everything supported? And most importantly, but sadly often not true, does it actually answer the question (even if the answer is that there is no answer)? You also need to watch out for spelling, grammar and punctuation errors, as well as continuing until the last second to improve the content and the expression. Don't waste time counting words.

There is no such thing as a perfect or model essay; flawed essays can gain full marks. There is always something more that could have been said, and examiners realise that students have limitations when writing under pressure in timed conditions. You are not penalised for what you didn't say in comparison to some idealised concept of the perfect answer, but are rewarded for the knowledge and

understanding you have shown. It is not as difficult as you may think to do well, provided that you know the text in detail and have sufficient essay-writing experience. Follow the process of **choose**, **underline**, **select**, **support**, **structure**, **write** and **check**, and you can't go far wrong.

Text Guidance

Contexts

Biographical context

Ian McEwan was born on 21 June 1948 in Aldershot. His father was an officer in the British army and as a result McEwan travelled extensively during his childhood. Some of his subsequent writing reflects places in which he spent time, for example *The Innocent* draws on a period in Berlin. He read English at Sussex University, and then took the MA course in Creative Writing, recently established at the University of East Anglia by Malcolm Bradbury and Angus Wilson. He has written substantial numbers of short stories, but is best known as a novelist. His first novel, *The Cement Garden*, was published in 1978; *Atonement* (2001) is his eighth novel, and his most recent novel to date, *Saturday*, was published in 2005. He has also written a number of plays, screenplays, a libretto and a children's book. He has received numerous awards for his work.

McEwan has been short-listed for the prestigious Booker Prize for fiction (now the Man Booker Prize) on several occasions: for *The Comfort of Strangers* in 1981, for *Atonement* in 2001 and for *Saturday* in 2005. Many commentators feel it is ironic that he was actually awarded this prize for *Amsterdam* in 1998, viewed by many as one of his least successful novels.

McEwan's early fiction is characterised by an interest in adolescent sexuality, including deviant variants of it. Later novels have been set in historical and/or precise geographical contexts, and have displayed an interest in psychology, medicine and unusual mental states.

McEwan has always been especially interested in the theoretical status of fiction, and many of his works are explicitly concerned with this issue. The critic Brian Finney comments: 'From his earliest collections of short stories Ian McEwan has consistently drawn attention to the status of his fiction as discourse by alluding to or parodying traditional literary **genres**, thereby forcing the reader to take note of the presence of a self conscious narrator.'

Historical context

Life in England in the 1930s and 1940s

The 1930s was an era of transition in English society. While many aspects of life were seemingly unchanged in essence since the Victorian period, a number of forces were at work that were fatally undermining the old order. These tendencies were either accelerated or held back by the war, but the net result was that after 1945 England changed in a number of fundamental respects. *Atonement* is firmly set in

the pre-1945 world, and there are various features that may be unfamiliar to a twenty-first-century reader.

The class system in England remained influential until the 1960s. Based upon medieval distinctions of wealth and occupation, by the interwar period it had taken the following form:

- **The aristocracy** were mostly hereditary, noble landowners, although the idea that this was therefore a fixed caste is misleading; families were ennobled in all ages, originally for military prowess, and more recently to reflect political achievement or commercial wealth. A code of noble behaviour was expected of members of this class. Lord Marshall's elevation for the sale of chocolate is a prime example of a middle-class industrial family joining the aristocracy.
- **The middle class** was a large grouping of people in very disparate positions, from junior clerk and shopkeeper at the bottom to professionals, landowners and industrialists at the top. What they had in common was a certain standard of living and a set of shared values and kinds of behaviour. The lower an individual's income level, the more important it was to conform to middle-class social norms in order to ensure acceptance; to be considered 'working class' was the worst fate that could befall a middle-class person. Self-restraint, politeness and good manners were key aspects of behaviour.
- **The working class** consisted of urban, industrial workers or manual workers, but a substantial minority were agricultural labourers. Although free education had been available for all classes since the late nineteenth century, levels of educational attainment among working-class children were generally low and their behaviour, as often exaggerated by the middle class, typically showed less restraint and greater enslavement by 'animal' desires.

The rise of the urban working class had led to significant changes in politics as support for socialism, the political movement seeking improved rights for workers, increased; the moderate Labour Party was founded in 1900 to represent the working classes in Parliament, and formed a government for the first time in 1924. Although the first Labour government was short-lived, it indicated that the interests of the working class were going to be an important consideration in politics in the future. A number of middle-class people and intellectuals were sympathetic to the socialist cause, believing that working-class people had been discriminated against for generations and deserved more equal treatment.

Domestic servants were common before the Second World War. Wealthier households usually employed one or two to perform menial duties before the introduction of labour-saving devices such as washing machines and vacuum cleaners. Larger houses provided accommodation for these servants, generally in the attic, and they mostly worked 'below stairs' in the basement. A 'green baize door' marked the boundary between the domain of the family and the area of the servants. The war

virtually ended the employment of domestic servants, except by the very wealthiest. In part the creation of the welfare state by the Labour government elected in 1945 made it unnecessary for people to undertake demeaning work for low salaries; in part the experience of the war made middle-class people more uncomfortable about employing servants. The arrival of new technology soon made them unnecessary.

The education system in the 1930s and 1940s offered free, compulsory education for all, but only up to the age of 14. Upper- and middle-class people chose to send their children — especially their sons — to private (independent) schools if they could. The motives were as much social as educational: at private school their offspring would mix only with children from similar social backgrounds. At the more prestigious schools, of which Eton and Roedean are prime examples, connections would be made that would improve the child's career opportunities in later life. In order to obtain entry into such a 'public school', the pupil would attend a 'prep (preparatory) school' between the ages of 7 and 13, and would have to pass the Common Entrance examination to the public school in question. There was a strict code of conduct among the pupils in such schools, which were generally highly snobbish; there was a hierarchy based upon the father's job and status, and even the number of initials a child had (more initials = more aristocratic). Bullying was endemic; pupils were often bullied for being academic, or for not being sporty enough, or for their physical appearance. It was part of the 'schoolboy code' never to 'tell tales' on anybody else, which was especially convenient for the bullies, who could therefore never be exposed and punished.

There was also an expectation, which the schools reinforced, that well brought-up boys were 'seen and not heard', would not speak to an adult without being invited to, and would generally conduct their relationships with adults — often including their own parents — with considerable formality. This form of upbringing contributed to the image of the typical English gentleman as being cold and emotionally repressed, with a 'stiff upper lip', i.e. they did not betray emotion by crying, as their sisters undoubtedly would; that would be 'sissy'.

The Second World War

The Second World War was the most destructive war in human history. During its course of nearly six years (1939–45) more than 55 million people perished, many times exceeding the horrors of the First World War (the 'Great War', 1914–18). Yet, for all that, attitudes to the Second World War remain curiously mixed. There has been an outpouring in recent years of popular historical works on the war, which have topped bestseller lists, a trend that shows no sign of abating; there has also been a resurgence of novels set during the conflict, of which *Atonement* is but one example. Why is this?

There are many possible answers to this question, and sociologists and cultural historians will no doubt debate them for years to come. Some relate to the unique nature of the conflict itself, involving as it did civilian populations in all the European combatant countries, and to the consequences of this experience for social cohesion and in the collective memory. Others relate to the clear moral dimension of the conflict: this was a war for principles, values and morality. The enemy was perceived as uniquely evil, and the confirmation of this with the exposure of the extermination camps in the closing days of the war cemented this idea in the popular imagination. Others again relate to the extraordinarily ambivalent attitudes held by many people, then and now, towards the whole phenomenon of Nazi Germany. Many recent historical studies now feel able to admit openly what has been unspoken for 60 years: the Wehrmacht (the German armed forces) was the outstanding military organisation of the war, out-performing every other participant to an unprecedented degree. Its most notorious arm, the Waffen SS (the military corps of the Nazi party), attracts adulation and revulsion in millions of people. It is no coincidence that the market for Wehrmacht memorabilia, and even more so for SS items, shows exceptional vitality, although a proportion of this interest is related to modern neo-Nazi political movements such as the National Front.

A further set of reasons for the current interest in the Second World War relates to the nature of the fighting: whereas the trench warfare of the First World War allowed no opening for tactical innovation or even, in any conventional sense, for heroism, the highly mobile warfare of the Second World War allowed brilliant generalship to be displayed (almost exclusively by the Germans) and led to tactical and strategic innovation on a huge scale. Battlefield casualties were low by the standards of the previous war, except on the Eastern Front (the war between Germany and the Soviet Union); Britain, for example, lost 326,000 men in combat, compared with 703,000 killed (and more than 1.6 million wounded) in the Great War. Those who fought in the war had a sense of purpose, and of the value of their contribution, which was not present in the First World War.

The background to the war has three aspects: first, the treatment that Germany received at the end of the First World War left the Germans deeply bitter and determined to overthrow the hated Versailles Treaty. Second, the Wall Street Crash in the USA in 1929 did severe damage to the economies of all the countries of Europe. The resulting social unrest threatened the fabric of societies throughout the continent and led to extreme, anti-democratic parties receiving wide support. The Nazi party in Germany came to power in the wake of the economic crisis. Third and most fundamentally, the war was about competing political ideologies. By the 1930s, three utterly irreconcilable sets of ideas were prevalent in western Europe about how societies should be organised, and how wealth and influence should be distributed:

- **Democracy**: the belief that all citizens should participate in choosing a government, and that all citizens should enjoy equal rights. This dominant philosophy was greatly weakened in the 1930s by the failure of democratic governments to deal with the consequences of the Wall Street Crash.

- **Communism**: this idealistic philosophy, created by Karl Marx and Friedrich Engels in their *Communist Manifesto* of 1848, had become a powerful alternative since the success of the Bolshevik revolution in Russia in 1917.
- **Fascism and Nazism**: anti-democratic movements, which were extremely nation-alistic, seeking to unite a nation rather than divide it as democracy was thought to. The individual was to be subordinated to the needs of the state; and in the Nazi version, was to play a role in the striving of mankind towards its destiny. The Nazi philosophy also included a vicious and spurious racism, which believed that the Germans were members of an 'Aryan' master race; all other races were viewed as inferior and, in the case of the Jews, sub-human.

The war commenced in September 1939 with the Nazi invasion of Poland. Britain sent a large part of its army to France as the British Expeditionary Force (BEF) in the autumn of 1939 to reinforce the French and to await the inevitable attack, which came in May 1940. The German tactic of Blitzkrieg (highly mobile warfare spearheaded by tanks) took the French by surprise. They were hampered by weak and divided Anglo-French leadership, and the Germans broke through immediately. The BEF made a fighting withdrawal to the port of Dunkirk, from where a large number of troops (more than 300,000) were successfully evacuated to Britain. France fell and came under German occupation, but in the ensuing Battle of Britain the fighters of the Royal Air Force held off the German Luftwaffe (air force). The planned German invasion of Britain was abandoned in September.

Thereafter, the British engaged the Germans in the deserts of North Africa, but until the Allied invasion of Normandy in June 1944 (D-Day) and the final push into Germany, the British could only attack Germany itself by air. The role of the RAF's Bomber Command was central: waves of bombers flew to Germany nightly, to bomb the cities and factories in the hope of breaking German civilian morale and damaging the productive capacity of German industry. Casualties among bomber aircrew were high, and the ever-present risk of being shot down over Germany meant either death or captivity as a prisoner of war.

The German invasion of the Soviet Union in June 1941 proved the turning point of the war, for Hitler had met his match in the leader of the Soviet Union, Stalin, and after nearly four years of often bestial fighting with huge casualties, the Russian Red Army struck into Berlin in late April 1945 and destroyed both Nazism and Germany.

In parallel with the war in Europe, a war in Asia developed following the unprovoked Japanese attack on the US fleet at Pearl Harbor in Hawaii in December 1941. This led to US involvement in the European theatre of war (the US Air Force made a major contribution to the bombing of Germany, and contributed the largest forces to D-Day and the subsequent campaign in western Europe). The war in Asia ended with the dropping of atomic bombs on the Japanese cities of Hiroshima and Nagasaki in August 1945.

The British army in the Second World War

It may be helpful for the reader to understand the structure and ranks of the army at the time. The British army has always maintained a fundamental distinction between officers and 'other ranks'. Officers took the 'King's Commission' and swore an oath of personal loyalty to the monarch. They were required to be gentlemen, and were bound by a strict code of conduct. They were therefore, in practice, invariably from the upper or middle classes. Aristocrats generally took commissions in the Guards or the Household Cavalry; middle-class officers led all the other regiments and units. The 'other ranks' were, in peacetime, recruited entirely from the working class. Although subject to a strict disciplinary code, they did not take a commission (indeed, senior 'other ranks' were known as 'Non-Commissioned Officers' or NCOs). NCOs wore their badge of rank on the sleeves of their tunics; officers wore them on their epaulettes.

Officer ranks

General (three levels)	commander of a division
Brigadier	commander of a brigade
Colonel/Lieutenant-Colonel	commanding officer of a regiment or battalion
Major	officer commanding a company or squadron
Captain	
Lieutenant/Second Lieutenant	

Other ranks

Regimental Sergeant-Major	crown
Company Sergeant-Major	crown
Sergeant	three stripes
Corporal	two stripes
Lance-Corporal	one stripe
Private	

The Second World War: the home front

The Second World War was 'total war' in a way that the Great War had not been. The development of medium-range bombers meant that all of Britain was within range of the Luftwaffe, operating from airfields in France and the Low Countries. Aerial bombing was viewed as a wonder weapon, which could destroy a country's ability to wage war as well as causing a political crisis by destroying the morale of the civilian population. The Blitz — the indiscriminate bombing of London by the Luftwaffe from the summer of 1940 onwards — became a powerful part of the myth of British fortitude during the war. The population of London experienced almost nightly bombing during extended periods of the war, and civilian casualties were high. The experience of night-time raids and of waiting fearfully in air-raid shelters (either communal, or the Anderson shelters built in back gardens) for the all-clear

to sound meant, at the very least, disturbed sleep patterns, not to mention the continuous climate of fear. Air-raid wardens watched for any breach of the blackout, which was designed to make the job of the enemy bombers harder but which became a daily irritation, especially as some wardens pursued their duties officiously. Many civilians played their part as wardens or fire-watchers, or in the fire service. The fear of a gas attack (as in the trenches during the First World War) led to the issue of gas masks to all civilians, and during the early years children were required to carry them everywhere in case of a surprise attack. People lived by the air-raid sirens — the wailing, which warned of a raid, and the continuous all-clear, which meant that the threat was over for a while.

Total war made itself felt in other areas as well. The entire economy was mobilised for the war effort and was subject to tight central control. Virtually all commodities were rationed; petrol was effectively unobtainable for private use. The labour market came under government control, and those young men who were not conscripted into the armed forces were required to do 'war work', as were a large number of women. The great majority of men aged between 18 and 41 served in the army, navy or air force. While many volunteered on the outbreak of war, those who were conscripted were initially enlisted as 'other ranks', whatever their background, with subsequent opportunities for appropriate candidates to become officers. This meant that the rigid class structure of the British forces was undermined for the duration of the war, as many men who at any other time would have become officers served in the ranks (Robbie Turner, a Cambridge graduate, is an example of this).

Many children were evacuated from the larger cities, especially London, and were billeted on unrelated families in safer country districts, leading in many cases to tension. Some were sent overseas to Canada and elsewhere for the duration of the war, and there were tragic cases of evacuee ships being torpedoed and sunk en route to their supposedly safer destinations.

Dunkirk and the fall of France

When war was declared, the decision was taken that the bulk of the British army would be deployed to France to defend against the expected German invasion. This force, ultimately of nine infantry divisions, was called the British Expeditionary Force, as its predecessor in the First World War had been. It was agreed that the BEF would come under French overall command. The refusal of the Belgian government to accept the inevitable and abandon its policy of neutrality prevented the British and French armies from preparing strong defensive positions in Belgium. The German army ignored Belgian neutrality, and when the Germans invaded Belgium the BEF had to advance rapidly into Belgium (on 10 May 1940) and was unable to prepare itself adequately before the German onslaught arrived. The French army performed poorly and collapsed in many places; although the BEF fought well, despite its lack of armour, it was quickly forced to withdraw back to France following the failure of the French formations flanking it. This led to the anger towards the French army displayed by the retreating British troops. It was not until 28 May that the BEF was officially ordered to withdraw to Dunkirk on the French coast, abandoning all its equipment in the process. By the end of 4 June, more than 338,000 troops had been successfully evacuated from Dunkirk in Operation 'Dynamo', but more than 100,000 troops were killed or captured in the futile campaign.

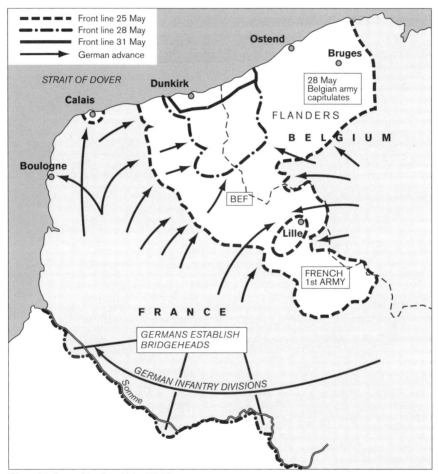

The withdrawal to Dunkirk, 1940

This, however, merely offered a breather to Britain, for the plans for the German invasion of Britain (Operation Seelöwe or Sealion) were ready, and the evacuated forces were expected to form up immediately for the defence of the homeland. Given that they had left all their artillery, vehicles and heavy weapons in France, the expectation was that they would be massacred by the Wehrmacht in a short period of time. This explains the mixed mood of Robbie (and the other survivors of Dunkirk) as depicted

in Part Three of *Atonement*: the evacuation from France was viewed as at best a temporary reprieve, and it was not until the autumn of 1940 that it became clear that the RAF's performance in the Battle of Britain had persuaded Hitler to call off Operation Sealion, and the invasion of Britain was no longer a possibility.

Literary context

The Second World War novel

Atonement is one of a large number of novels set in, or including, the Second World War. 'Historical' novels have always been popular, but in many cases the historical setting has merely lent colour to an otherwise unremarkable story. The particular attraction of the Second World War as a context for contemporary novelists, apart from the fact that many of them lived through it, is the extraordinarily rich range of experiences it offered. No other conflict, arguably no other period in history, impacted upon the lives of so many people in such a memorable or devastating way. It was 'total war' as no previous war had been, in the sense that civilian populations were directly targeted for indiscriminate bombing and were profoundly affected by rationing, evacuation and conscription for military or civilian service.

Significant novels about the Second World War began to be published soon after it ended. A model that became increasingly common was for the war to act as the culmination of a story that started during the interwar years. This allowed the novelist to show how characters were changed by the experiences of war, which typically heightened feelings and reactions and frequently involved tragedy. In novels set in peacetime, the death of younger characters can generally only be secured by crime or freak accident, whereas in the Second World War death was so common, from such a range of causes, that it can become a convenient plot device.

Evelyn Waugh's *Brideshead Revisited*, published as early as 1945, allows the reader to see how its spoilt characters respond to the hardships of war. The war section in Anthony Powell's great novelistic sequence *A Dance to the Music of Time* (1951–75) has the same effect. Evelyn Waugh's magisterial *Sword of Honour* trilogy (1952–61) is set entirely during the war, as are Olivia Manning's Balkan and Levant trilogies (1960–80). More recently, many novelists have set works in this period; for example, Louis de Bernières's *Captain Corelli's Mandolin* (1994) explores the conflict of loyalties that develops when a member of an occupying army becomes emotionally involved with a local woman; Sebastian Faulks's *Charlotte Gray* (1999) examines the role of British agents sent into occupied France.

While some Second World War novels have concerned themselves directly with combatants and combat, others have focused on civilians and how the war affected them. Helen Dunmore's *The Siege* (2001), for example, examines the fate of Russian civilians during the epic siege of Leningrad from 1941 to 1944.

The Second World War changed British society in a number of ways, which novelists have observed and recorded. Life in the 1930s was seen as carefree and, often, irresponsible; the advent of war, bringing rationing and shared suffering, caused everyone to 'pull together' for the common good. Gerald Durrell's *My Family and Other Animals* (1956), for example, records a peacetime idyll destroyed by the outbreak of war. There was also, during a war that lasted nearly six years, considerable paranoia about enemy spies. *Carrie's War* (1973) by Nina Bawden examines what it was like to be a child in wartime England, as does John Boorman's great film *Hope and Glory* (1987). In *The English Patient* (1992) by Michael Ondaatje, the innocent multinational team of geographers working to map Egypt's western desert is tragically broken apart by the forces of war.

The coming of age novel

The transition from childhood to adulthood, via the stressful interlude of adolescence, is a period that is engraved in the memories of most adults. It is during this time that life-changing experiences are undergone, and in many cases the character of the adult is determined by especially significant, traumatic or transcendental experiences. It has been a focus of attention for many writers, and there are innumerable novels, poems and plays explicitly addressing this absorbing and universal theme. *Atonement* may be seen as a 'coming of age' novel because it is centrally concerned with a protagonist on the cusp of adolescence who finds herself in a situation which she cannot quite understand, and her immature responses have immediate and devastating consequences for the adults directly concerned. What equally interests McEwan are the more subtle long-term consequences for the central child–adolescent as she comes to appreciate the significance of what she has done, apparently in all innocence. What places this novel firmly in this category is that it is not dealing with a child who could not be expected to have any notion of the consequences of her actions. The whole point about the 'coming-of-age' moment is that the characters *do*, dimly and intermittently, perceive the adult dimension, and are at times stricken with uncertainty or confusion, so that when they eventually realise the damage they have caused, it comes not as a bolt from the blue but as confirmation of what they have increasingly, and with sickening guilt, feared was or might be the case.

Although there are innumerable earlier examples of novels in this **genre**, including Dickens's *Great Expectations*, perhaps the most obviously relevant is L. P. Hartley's *The Go-Between*, published in 1953 but set in the summer of the year 1900. It can be seen as the prototype of *Atonement* in that the impressionable young character, probably turning from 12 to 13, is used as a lovers' go-between by adults who can be viewed as cynically taking advantage of the naivety of the child (and so, arguably, can be seen as receiving their just deserts for such manipulation), and also in that the momentous events occur during a memorable summer.

The latter seems to be a motif of special significance for British authors; because the British weather is so depressingly grey and wet for so much of the year, a brief and glorious summer often stands out in the memory as a uniquely blessed time. Seen nostalgically through rose-tinted vision, all the summers of one's childhood are remembered as sunnier than they actually were. For such a time to be associated with coming of age, rites of passage or some form of initiation into the adult world makes it especially resonant. It is also the only time of the year when children are free for an extended period of time, during the long summer holiday, and when the weather allows them to be out of the house. It is the end of the school year in Britain too, so the changes that occur in a long summer are reinforced by a new status on returning to school. There is also the comparison with nature: summer is the season of development and maturation, of coming into full blossom before decay sets in during the autumn. Laurie Lee's *Cider With Rosie* (1959) is another example of a novel that enshrines this time of transition.

It is perhaps worth noting that this transition from child to adult has been marked by formal rituals, trials and celebrations in virtually all primitive civilisations throughout history (but without the 'adolescent' or 'teenager' stage, which is a post-war marketing invention; prior to this, children modelled themselves on adults in their beliefs, dress and lifestyle). It is arguable that it is the absence of such recognised structures in modern Western societies that renders the emerging adult peculiarly sensitive to life-changing events at this time. What is notable about *The Go-Between* is the author's clear indication that the events of that faraway summer have scarred the young Leo so permanently that he is unable to grow up into a fully independent adult or to form adult relationships. McEwan's Briony also records a life wracked by guilt for the consequences of her actions and dominated by the atonement that she felt she must make.

Postmodernism

'Modernism' is the general term applied to the literary (and artistic) movements of the first half of the twentieth century. Modernist literature typically experiments with form, depends on symbol and myth as structural principles, and explores the workings of the unconscious mind as a result of the influence of Freudian analysis. The 'stream of consciousness' mode arose to capture the flux and development within individual thought and to convey the complexity and instability of personality. Modernist texts looked back to mythology for parallels for the individual beleaguered by social expectations and threatened by the ending of an era; the *Odyssey* motif (as in James Joyce's *Ulysses*) was thought particularly appropriate to represent the difficult and changing journey of life.

Postmodernism, which succeeded it in the later twentieth century, shares the preoccupations of Modernism but goes further in that it mocks and rejects traditional linear narrative and refuses to give the reader the comfort of **closure**. Central to Postmodernist writing is the author's aim of unsettling and deconstructing (critically analysing) accepted notions about language, about identity, about writing itself. It tends to cross the dividing line between high and popular culture, and it exposes and discredits previously accepted attitudes to female, colonial, religious and political oppression. It is **self-reflexive** in calling attention to the way it has come into existence and to its own nature as something that has been deliberately constructed. As a consequence, it makes us reflect on writing in general and on the triple relationship between author, character and reader. Questions of identity in Postmodernist fiction are created by parallelism, binary oppositions, doublings, mixing fictional and historical characters, twisting well-known myths, and drawing attention to the artificiality of all representation.

Postmodernism is based on the premise that language is ultimately an unstable and unreliable medium of communication, yet ironically still uses language to tell us so (as summed up in the conundrum of whether we can believe the Cretan who says 'All Cretans are liars'). It proves the impossibility of reducing a text to a single truth, in order to cast doubt on the possibility of defining such concepts as history. Borrowings from earlier texts set up echoes and also show us the blind spots of these earlier texts. Postmodernist writing is therefore built on ambivalence and is funda-mentally paradoxical. It asserts and then subversively undermines such abstract principles as value, order, meaning, control, certainty, morality — in the process undermining itself and any tendency to consistency or a single interpretation.

Because large-scale historical interpretations, such as Marxism, have enslaved large parts of the world in the past by being absolute and universal, the Postmodernist writer suggests that small-scale, modest, local narratives are needed to replace them and to restore humanity. We need provisional, little stories that are strong enough to guide us but make no claims beyond the here and now.

It is possible to convey story and history in other ways than the standard narration technique of omniscient narrator writing in the past tense with interludes of character dialogue. A Postmodernist text is a collage that reveals that there are many ways of seeing, depending on who you are, where you are looking from, and what your social and historical experience is.

The main issues to be aware of when dealing with contemporary texts and Postmodernist critical theory are:

- **Plurality**: because texts can be read in different ways by different readers at different times and in different contexts, there is never a single meaning or a single 'right answer' that can be taught and learned. Readers must learn how to reach their own conclusions about texts and writers, taking account of other interpretations in the process.
- **Intertextuality**: writers do not write, nor do readers read, in a literary vacuum. The relationships between texts, and the comparisons that can be drawn between them, illuminate the writing and reading. This is why it is now a requirement for all A-level English Literature specifications to contain comparative study of whole texts.

- **Contextuality**: again, writers write and readers read within a number of contexts: social, cultural and historical. These affect the ways in which texts can be read. Candidates at AS must show their awareness of these influences, while at A2 they should be able to evaluate the significance of contexts for the way in which texts are read.

Atonement clearly falls within the definition of Postmodernist texts, because the author refuses to write a conventional narrative (see, especially, 'Viewpoint and voice' and 'Postmodernism and intertextuality' on pp. 77–87 of this guide).

Chapter summaries and commentary

Part One: Chapters 1 to 14: pp. 3–187   [1935, Surrey]
Part Two: no chapters: pp. 191–265   [1940, France]
Part Three: no chapters: pp. 269–349   [1940, London]
'London, 1999': no chapters: pp. 353–72

Part One: pp. 3–187

Part One is set in the country house of the Tallis family in Surrey one day during the summer of 1935. It consists of 14 numbered chapters, each apparently told in the past tense by a range of omniscient narrators, although we know that they were all 'in fact' written by Briony some years after the events took place.

One: 1 (pp. 3–17) — voice of Briony

Chapter 1 commences with Briony's play and quickly introduces 'her cousins from the distant north' (p. 3) and 'her brother'. The first event is Emily Tallis reading her daughter's play, indulging Briony, whose transition from child to adolescent is explicitly signed: 'ah, that hot smooth little body she remembered from its infancy, and still not gone from her, not quite yet' (p. 4). Briony admits to her 'luminous, yearning fantasies' (p. 4) — including describing herself as (in elder brother Leon's imagined words) 'my younger sister, Briony Tallis the writer' (p. 4). Briony's bossy interest in the behaviour of her elder siblings is made clear in her (improper) concern for brother Leon's behaviour: she hoped to 'guide him away from his careless succession of girlfriends' (p. 4).

There follows a long description of Briony, and the background to the play (pp. 4–8).

The cousins arrive (p. 9) and 'Hardman's son Danny' makes an appearance.

Briony muses on the difficulties of casting, and after an afternoon by the pool the Quinceys report for a rehearsal. Lola overcomes the hostility of the twins by evoking 'The Parents' — a curious phrase (p. 12). Briony's naivety and self-centredness are illustrated: 'it had never occurred to her that her cousins would not want to play their parts in *The Trials of Arabella*' (p. 12). Lola seizes the initiative and demands to play Arabella; Briony is mortified, but after briefly wallowing in self-pity she fights back. The rehearsal begins.

References and allusions

p. 4, *The Trials of Arabella*. Arabella was the sister of the **eponymous** heroine of Richardson's novel *Clarissa*, which Cecilia is spending the summer reading (see p. 25) and in which Clarissa is raped.

p. 9, re-armament. In 1935 Adolf Hitler had been in power in Germany for two years already and had recently announced that Germany would re-arm in breach of the terms of the Treaty of Versailles. Informed people in Britain were already talking of re-armament and a possible war.

p. 9, the Abyssinia question. In the summer of 1935 Benito Mussolini, the Italian Fascist leader, invaded the independent country of Abyssinia; it was incorporated into the Italian Empire the following year.

One: 2 (pp. 18–31) — voice of Cecilia

The next morning Cecilia brings in wild flowers and puts them in the Meissen vase for the guest room. Desperate for a cigarette, she goes out through the French windows to where Robbie is smoking by the fountain. They talk, and there is immediately tension. She has brought the vase out to fill it with water from the fountain. As she does so, Robbie intervenes, and accidentally breaks two pieces off the vase, which fall into the fountain. To prevent him from retrieving them, Cecilia strips to her underwear, steps into the fountain and retrieves the missing pieces. Angry, she returns to the house.

References and allusions

p. 18, Bernini's *Triton*. The Triton fountain in the Piazza Barberini (see p. 314) in Rome, sculpted by Gianlorenzo Bernini in 1642–43, is considered one of the glories of Italian Baroque sculpture: the copy in the garden of the Tallis house is evidence of the fashion for Italianate decoration in eighteenth-century England. It is presumably a left-over from the original 'Adam-style' (see p. 19) house.

p. 19, squat, lead-paned baronial Gothic. The house dates from the late nineteenth century, the end of the Victorian era, when the Gothic style dominated architecture. This was characterised by fake-medieval details, pointed arches and windows divided into small panes by lead dividers.

p. 19, Pevsner. Sir Nikolaus Pevsner (1902–83), a Russian-German Jewish refugee from Germany who arrived in Britain in 1935, was a brilliant architectural historian

who was responsible for the seminal *Buildings of England* series, published from 1951 on, in which he evaluated everything of architectural interest in England, paying particular attention to country houses. The Tallis house would have been condemned for being tasteless and derivative.

p. 19, Adam-style. Robert Adam (1728–92) was the greatest architect of country houses in the golden age of such buildings in the eighteenth century. His 'classical', Italianate style was based upon the work of the architect Palladio.

p. 19, Friesians. A breed of cow widely raised in England.

p. 20, Chesterfields. 'Chesterfield' is a style of heavily padded leather armchairs and sofas, popular in Victorian England and typically found in country houses.

p. 21, *Clarissa*. A novel by Samuel Richardson, written in 1747–48. Although Cecilia finds it heavy going, Robbie is (revealingly) more appreciative of it; the plot centres around the rape of Clarissa, from which she never recovers.

p. 23, Verdun. The epic battle of Verdun, which lasted from February to December 1916, was one of the most destructive engagements in the First World War. The German army launched attacks on this key French fortress; by the end of the year, one million men had become casualties, but Verdun did not fall.

p. 24, Meissen. The porcelain made in the eastern German town of Meissen is considered to be the finest in the world. The factory began to manufacture hard-clay porcelain items in 1710 in imitation of Chinese originals.

p. 25, Bolshevik cigarettes. Cecilia has already commented that Robbie used to roll cigarettes when he tried being a Communist (p. 22). 'Bolsheviks' is what the Russian communists called themselves.

p. 27, not that they actually awarded degrees to women anyway. Although the first college for women at Cambridge University was founded in 1869 (Girton College, which Cecilia attended), women were not officially awarded degrees by the university until 1947. They were allowed to sit the examinations, though, which is how Cecilia knows that she only achieved a Third Class degree, compared with Robbie's First.

One: 3 (pp. 32–42) — voice of Briony

The same morning, Briony directs rehearsals, commenting on 'the morning's colossal heat' (p. 35). During a break, she looks out of the window — and witnesses Cecilia undressing, apparently at Robbie's bidding, then immersing herself in the pool.

There then follows a key section in which a later Briony analyses the change that the child undergoes at this point — and gives a hint about the authorship of this text; but saying 'Six decades later she would describe how at the age of thirteen…' (p. 41) is extremely self-referential when it is part of that very description from six decades later. Nevertheless, this is the point at which an acute reader may begin to ask questions about the status of the text and the narration.

This is surely one of the themes of the work:

> Unseen, from two storeys up, with the benefit of unambiguous sunlight, she had privileged access across the years to adult behaviour, to rites and conventions she knew nothing about, as yet....Briony had her first, weak intimation that for her now it could no longer be fairy-tale castles and princesses, but the strangeness of the here and now, of what passed between people, the ordinary people that she knew, and what power one could have over the other, and how easy it was to get everything wrong, completely wrong. (p. 39)

She claims that this helped her 'to arrive at an impartial psychological realism, which she had discovered for herself, one special morning during a heat wave in 1935' (p. 41). At this point in the narrative, however, she makes no reference to the price she had to pay for this achievement.

One: 4 (pp. 43–54) — voice of Cecilia

On the afternoon of the same day: Cecilia has repaired the vase, but before she can take it up to Paul Marshall's room, she meets Briony, who has abandoned the play — but will not explain why coherently. From Marshall's room Cecilia sees Briony run over to the Temple on the island, and then sees Leon and Paul arrive in Hardman's trap and speak to Robbie. She comes down and meets them in the hall. 'All day long, she realised, she had been feeling strange, and seeing strangely, as though everything was already long in the past' (p. 48). (Cecilia observes, a propos of nothing, that she has observed Danny Hardman hanging around the children, especially Lola, p. 48.)

They sit by the pool and Marshall delivers a **monologue** about his company's new chocolate bar, the Amo bar. Dull as he is, Cecilia nevertheless fantasises about marrying him, and when she likens his ear-hair to 'pubic hair' (p. 50) it is clear that she is in an excited state. Leon states that he had met Robbie on the way in (as Cecilia saw) and invited him to dinner. Cecilia is furious but cannot say why. Again, she feels unreal (p. 53).

References and allusions

p. 46, Girton. Cecilia's college at Cambridge (see note to p. 27 above).

p. 50, Pass the Amo! 'Ammo' is army slang for ammunition, so this is a clever marketing phrase linking the new bar with the essential role of ammunition in an army; it is also a reminder of the Latin word 'amo', meaning 'I love', as every prep school boy would know.

p. 50, Mr Hitler. It seems quaint to see Adolf Hitler, the Nazi dictator of Germany and architect of the Second World War, referred to as 'Mr Hitler', but the usage was normal at the time.

p. 50, general conscription. Service in the armed forces was voluntary, but during the First World War compulsory military service, known in Britain as conscription,

had been introduced. There was an expectation that it would be reintroduced in the near future in preparation for a new war.

p. 52, her Roedean chums. Roedean School, in Brighton, is one of the most socially exclusive independent boarding schools for girls, much favoured by upper-middle-class families.

One: 5 (pp. 55–62) — voice of Lola (with exceptions)

The cousins do not understand why Briony suddenly abandons the rehearsals, but Lola wanders by chance into Paul's room and sees his luggage. Later, back in the nursery, Jackson mentions the word 'divorce' in connection with their parents. Paul Marshall appears at the door, chats with the twins and flirts with Lola.

Note that the perspective is inconsistent in this chapter — there is a section on p. 60 that is written from Marshall's point of view (giving essential information about his attitudes), which Lola could not have known.

One: 6 (pp. 63–71) — voice of Emily Tallis

Withdrawing to her cool, dark bedroom after lunch, seeking to avoid a migraine, Emily reflects on Leon, Cecilia, Briony, herself, and the cousins. She hears 'a little squeal of laughter abruptly smothered' (p. 69) and concludes that it is Lola and Marshall in the nursery.

Why does she not question this? It is the only evidence for what happens between them after the twins have been summoned for their bath.

References and allusions
p. 64, the cosy jargon of Cecilia's Cambridge. Emily is confused about 'gyp', which is Cambridge slang for a servant (probably derived from 'jupeau', the short skirt worn by kitchen servants, rather than from 'gypsy'); a 'set' is a set of rooms. The 'Little-Go' was the entrance test.

One: 7 (pp. 72–7) — voice of Briony

The chapter begins with a description of the neo-Greek temple on the artificial island and its history. Briony is slashing at nettles, venting her anger at Lola, the twins, plays and finally her childhood, indulging in yet another self-glorifying fantasy. Afterwards, in a strange mood, she resolves to wait on the bridge 'until events, real events, not her own fantasies, rose to her challenge, and dispelled her insignificance' (p. 77) — which they do, with a vengeance.

References and allusions
p. 72, Nicholas Revett. A celebrated architect (1721–1804) who studied the temples of ancient Athens and designed replicas of them for English country houses.

One: 8 (pp. 78–95) — voice of Robbie

Robbie, lying in the bath in the roof space of the bungalow he inhabits with his mother, relives his memories of Cecilia emerging from the fountain. He also retells the story of his parents' wedding and separation. He realises, belatedly, that he is in love with Cecilia, and types her a letter of apology for his behaviour of the morning. After several attempts he arrives at a final version — and then types an erotic postscript, perhaps influenced by 'the page at which his *Anatomy* tended to fall open these days' (p. 85). He writes a sanitised version longhand, but does not put it in an envelope immediately. After bathing and hastily scooping up a letter, he walks to the house; seeing Briony on the bridge, he gives her the letter to give to Cecilia — and realises, too late, that he has put the obscene one into the envelope.

There is extensive analysis of Robbie and his aspirations in this chapter; it is ironic that he has just discovered love, just discovered freedom and has chosen his own path at last.

References and allusions

p. 78, a Fauvist. Fauvism was an art movement at the beginning of the twentieth century in France.

p. 82, Auden, Housman. Fashionable, romantic poets; both were homosexual.

p. 82, *Twelfth Night*, Malvolio. Malvolio is the malevolent (same word) character in Shakespeare's *Twelfth Night* who is hopelessly in love with Olivia — an apt parallel?

p. 82, *belle époque*. The period from 1890 to 1914, often known as the Golden Age of fashion; literally means 'the beautiful era'.

p. 83, verdigris. A blue-green coating that forms on copper when exposed to the air for a long time; evidence of ageing.

p. 83, oast house. A distinctive kind of building found in Kent, used for drying hops, from which beer is brewed.

p. 83, Romany. Describes travelling people, who used to be known as 'gypsies'; these stylistic touches were thought to be reminiscent of traveller costume.

p. 84, the hydraulics of Versailles. The Palace of Versailles had an advanced hydraulic system that linked 32 of the fountains.

p. 84, Le Nôtre. André Le Nôtre (1613–1700) was a celebrated French architect who designed the gardens of the Palace of Versailles.

p. 84, Freud. Sigmund Freud (1856–1939) was the father of modern psychiatry; he was celebrated for emphasising the central role of sexuality in human life.

p. 84, Petrarch. Francesco Petrarca (1304–74), an Italian poet, who invented the sonnet and wrote memorable love poems to a young woman named Laura.

p. 84, *Romaunt of the Rose*. A medieval **romance**; one of the earliest love poems.

p. 86, charlady. A woman employed as a cleaner.

p. 87, tied cottage. A cottage provided for an employee, often a domestic servant, by their employer. If the employment ceased, the accommodation had to be given up.

One: 9 (pp. 96–112) — voice of Cecilia

Cecilia, in her room, is trying to dress for dinner: each time, she is dissatisfied by what she sees in the mirror in the corridor. At the third attempt, she is hijacked by the miserable twins and helps them sort out their chaotic bedroom, borrowing socks for them from Briony's room. Going down to the kitchen, she defuses a row between Emily and Betty — Emily wanted the roast turned into a salad because of the heat. Finally she gets out onto the terrace and has a drink and a smoke with Leon. Eventually Briony appears; they go in, Briony embraces Leon, gives the letter to Cecilia — without the envelope — and Cecilia's reaction is '*Of course, of course*. How had she not seen it? Everything was explained' (p. 111). Now she understands why she has been feeling so strange all day; and she also realises that Briony must have read the letter.

References and allusions
p. 104, Gloucester Old Spot. A well-known breed of black and white pig.

One: 10 (pp. 113–24) — voice of Briony

Briony, in her room, having read the letter in the hall, reflects on the word she has never come across, and concludes that Cecilia needs her protection. She is determined to turn the day's events into a new, adult fiction — but does not know where to start. Lola comes in, upset; she claims that the twins have been bullying her. To distract her, Briony tells her of the letter — and Lola describes Robbie as a 'maniac'. Finally going downstairs, Briony hears noises from the library and, entering, sees Robbie and Cecilia embracing — which she interprets as him assaulting her. Embarrassed, they both leave.

One: 11 (pp. 125–44) — voice of Robbie

The dinner party: the wine is unsuitable; no-one wants the roast; the atmosphere is oppressive — there is an 'effect of suffocation' (p. 125).

Robbie fills in the missing part of the action, which is actually the missing chapter told in real time. He and Cecilia go into the library, and, slowly, come together. They are both virgins, but he is inside her when Briony enters and destroys everything. He understands:

> He saw it clearly, how it had happened: she had opened a sealed envelope to read his note and been disgusted, and in her obscure way felt betrayed. She had come looking for her sister — no doubt with the exhilarated notion of protecting her, or admonishing her, and had heard a noise from behind the closed library door. Propelled from the depths of her ignorance, silly imagining and girlish rectitude, she had come to a halt.…It was over. (p. 139)

Back at the dinner party, Briony sees that the twins are wearing her missing socks. 'You really are a tiresome little prima donna,' says Cecilia (p. 140). 'At this stage in her life Briony inhabited an ill-defined transitional space between the nursery and adult worlds which she crossed and recrossed unpredictably' (p. 141). The twins leave; Briony points out Lola's wounds, which she believes them to be responsible for, and there is commotion. Then Briony finds the letter left by the twins: they have run away. Instantly, the party breaks up to go out and search in the dark for them. Cecilia goes with Leon, Briony and Marshall go their own ways, and Robbie goes out alone as well — 'This decision, as he was to acknowledge many times, transformed his life' (p. 144).

The reader may feel it unlikely that Robbie could really have worked out so perceptively at the time what must have gone through Briony's mind. They may suspect, here if not earlier, that this may be the later work of Briony, attributing it to him.

References and allusions
p. 125, in the style of Gainsborough. Again (as with 'Adam-style', p. 19, p. 145), the Tallis painting is only 'in the style of' the great and fashionable Thomas Gainsborough (1727–88), whose portraits of the nobility hang in all the best-known country houses. It is revealing that 'No one knew who these people were' (p. 126); it is part of the illusion that the Tallis family is grander and older than it really is.
p. 128, Spode. A fashionable and expensive brand of fine bone china.
p. 128, a 1921 Barsac. An expensive, vintage, sweet dessert wine, wholly inappropriate to accompany such a meal, evidence of the family's inadequacy as hosts; 'the Old Man' will be angry at the wasting of such a rare wine in such a way.
p. 132, Orioli edition of *Lady Chatterley's Lover*. D. H. Lawrence's explicit novel about forbidden cross-class sex could not initially be published in Britain (it was finally published as late as 1960), so the first edition was published by Giuseppe Orioli in Florence in 1928.
p. 132, Soho. Often regarded as a seedy area of London where, from the nineteenth century onwards, prostitutes worked and writers and artists socialised. It would have been the best place to buy a banned book in the 1930s.

One: 12 (pp. 145–55) — voice of Emily

Emily, left alone in the house, reflects on how impossible Hermione (Lola's mother, her sister) was as a child, and how Lola is just as attention-seeking; and of how Jack is deceiving her, never coming home. She sits and reflects for half an hour. Jack phones, and is concerned to hear about the twins; then Leon, Cecilia, Briony and Lola enter, in distress; Leon speaks to Jack, and insists that Emily sit down before he breaks the news.

References and allusions
p. 145, Adam-style. Robert Adam (1728–92) was the greatest architect of country houses in England. The original house was in the style of Adam, but by an inferior architect (see also note to p. 19).

p. 145, fire dogs. Also known as 'andirons', these vaguely dog-shaped iron bars support the end of a log in an open fire.

p. 151, ceanothus. A shrub with striking dark blue flowers.

p. 151, wisteria. A purple-flowered climbing plant with a strong smell, much loved by the owners of country houses.

p. 155, Bakelite. The distinctive hard plastic used for telephone receivers in the interwar period.

One: 13 (pp. 156–72) — voice of Briony

Briony's chapter, the heart of the book, begins: 'Within the half hour Briony would commit her crime' (p. 156). She crosses the bridge, intending to go down to the temple on the island, but, once down there, what she thought was a bush separates into two and she sees the man run off. Lola is distraught; Briony is certain it was Robbie, but Lola claims never to have seen her assailant and does not argue. 'Nothing much was ever required of Lola after that' (p. 167). Briony's state of mind is extensively analysed immediately afterwards: 'What she meant was rather more complex than what everyone else so eagerly understood' (p. 169). Then they try to walk, just as Leon and Cecilia arrive on the road above.

Note how Briony repeatedly refers to Robbie as 'the maniac' — to reinforce the stereo-typing — and her real interest is in describing everything, writing and capturing it. Note also how often it sounds like Briony's subsequent reconstruction. The narrator refers, already, to 'the truth' that Lola kept quiet about (p. 168), reinforcing the retro-spective nature of the narration. Note also how flat the telling of the actual central event is.

One: 14 (pp. 173–87) — voice of Briony

The aftermath: the voice is Briony's again, recalling now 'her own vile excitement' (p. 173). The police arrive, and Briony exults in telling her story; then on a sudden impulse she runs up to Cecilia's bedroom and finds Robbie's letter in a drawer (p. 177) and hands it to the police inspector. Emily insists on seeing it; Cecilia is furious and leaves. Briony stays up all night, and is formally interviewed: 'I saw him,' she says. Jack's car breaks down and he remains absent.

In the morning, a figure is glimpsed, and they all go outside to confront him: Robbie has found the missing twins and is leading them home, one on his shoulders, the other beside him. But because this is Briony's chapter (and Briony's story), and she is at last sent to bed, we do not witness what follows, and when, an hour later, Robbie is led out to the police Humber in handcuffs, the events are witnessed silently by Briony from her bedroom window. Cecilia comes out, and there is an encounter which Briony cannot report; they drive off, but Grace Turner tries to stop the car, hitting it with her umbrella, calling them 'Liars' as they vanish from sight.

Briony's use of the phrase 'her own vile excitement' is the first really judgemental statement, and strengthens the reader's suspicion about the retrospective character of the narrative.

References and allusions
p. 173, a Humber. A make of car popular between the wars; senior police officers invariably arrived in a black Humber car in this period.

Part Two: voice of Robbie throughout

Note that there are no named or numbered sections.

Two: pp. 191–201

Initially the voice, situation and location are unspecified. It turns out to be Robbie, the voice is his only, written in the past tense but telling the story in real time. It is quickly seen as wartime, but not initially where; he is with two corporals, who call him 'Guv'nor' (p. 192). Robbie Turner is finally named at the top of p. 193, after it is revealed that he has been wounded in the side. He is leading Corporals Nettle and Mace, although he is only a private, by natural leadership. They are 'townies' (p. 193) and cannot read a map. The sense of futility and breakdown is already apparent, although not yet explained. (The setting is identified as 'French countryside' at the top of p. 194.) A boy's leg in a tree unnerves him. They arrive at a farm, and set up in the barn. The old woman's two sons, Henri and Jean-Marie Bonnet, bring a small feast for them. Finally he reveals that they are 'walking cross-country to Dunkirk' (p. 200). Henri movingly summarises the situation in France (p. 201).

Note that the chapter (and hence Part Two) commences with 'There were horrors enough' — an indication of the tone of what is to follow.

References and allusions
p. 191, the West Kents. There are, inevitably, many military references and slang terms in this section. The West Kents were an infantry regiment. The British army traditionally recruited in individual counties and cities, and formed units, especially of infantry, of people from the same area.
p. 193, he didn't even have a single stripe. Non-Commissioned Officers (NCOs) carried badges showing their ranks on the sleeves of their tunics. One stripe denoted a lance-corporal, two stripes a corporal and three stripes a sergeant. A private had no stripes.
p. 196, RASC. The Royal Army Service Corps, responsible for transport and supply.
p. 196, Heal's. A celebrated department store in Tottenham Court Road, London, specialising in furniture and interior fittings.

p. 197, Mosley. Oswald Mosley (1896–1980) was the founder and leader of the British Union of Fascists (known as the 'blackshirts' because of their uniform), a party based on Mussolini's Fascists in Italy. It gained some working-class support during the 1930s, but the party was banned and Mosley was imprisoned after the outbreak of war.

p. 200, Stuka. The Junkers Ju. 87 Stuka was the first successful dive bomber in Europe. It delivered a 1,000-pound bomb with devastating accuracy because the pilot put the aircraft into a near-vertical dive over the target, pulling up as he released the bomb. The air-brakes under the wing contributed to a distinctive, terrifying, banshee-like wailing as the aircraft attacked. They induced terror in their victims.

Two: pp. 202–13

Lying unsleeping, Robbie remembers three and a half years of prison (so now we know he was convicted, in November 1935). Even France is better than that (he had volunteered for the infantry to get out of prison). And he has something to get back for (we infer it is Cecilia). He has all 'her' letters in his greatcoat. It transpires he had only met her once — 'Six days out of prison, one day before he reported for duty' (p. 204) — in a Joe Lyons tea house in the Strand, in 1939. They had written to each other throughout the three and a half years, mostly in code; she had trained as a nurse. The meeting had not been easy: 'This moment had been imagined and desired for too long, and could not measure up' (p. 205). 'Everything they had, rested on a few minutes in a library years ago' (pp. 205–6); but when she left, at the bus stop, they kissed — 'a memory in the bank' (p. 206) — and he went off to training.

Now they can write regularly without censorship, but they are cautious about excessive intimacy. He finds the army more pleasant than prison. A letter from Cecilia (p. 209) summarises her view of her family (and her certainty that it was Danny Hardman who committed the rape). They had planned a holiday in Wiltshire — but war broke out, and they were unable to meet. From France, he attempts to persuade her to get in touch with her family again. In the last letter to reach him, in spring 1940, Cecilia reveals that Briony has refused to take up her place at Cambridge, and is training to be a nurse ('as a sort of penance', Cecilia thinks, p. 212). She wants to meet Cecilia, who thinks Briony may intend to withdraw her evidence.

As he lies thinking, Robbie recalls the key utterance of Cecilia, which has given him hope: 'I'll wait for you. Come back' (pp. 202–03). Although italicised, the context of its utterance is not immediately given, but it becomes a motif for this section of the book, being repeated several times before it is finally revealed (on p. 265) that this was what Cecilia said when Robbie was arrested. Cecilia herself repeated it in her first letter to Robbie in France ('She was quoting herself. She knew he would remember', p. 210).

References and allusions

p. 202, RA. The Royal Artillery, the gunners.

p. 203, *In the nightmare of the dark, All the dogs of Europe bark.* A line from W. H. Auden's poem 'In Memory of W. B. Yeats'.

p. 204, Tristan and Isolde etc. These are all references to celebrated pairs of literary lovers, several of them tragic. They are examples of the **intertextual** nature of the novel (see 'Postmodernism and intertextuality').

p. 207, the 'bull'. The trivial rules that all soldiers were required to follow, especially involving keeping uniforms clean and boots polished.

p. 208, Munich. In September 1938, the then British Prime Minister, Neville Chamberlain, had flown to Munich for negotiations with Hitler over the fate of the Sudetenland, a part of Czechoslovakia that Germany wished to annex. Britain (and France) had agreed to allow Hitler to do this (this was the doomed policy known as 'appeasement') and Chamberlain had claimed on his return to Britain that this meant 'peace in our time'. Many people did not believe him.

p. 210, British Expeditionary Force. The BEF was the name given to the British army that fought in France and the Low Countries throughout the First World War (1914–18), and the use of the same name perhaps suggested that the War Office thought that this war might be a re-run. As it was, the BEF was retreating to the Channel within weeks of the German invasion (see the section on Dunkirk and the fall of France on pp. 22–24 of this guide).

Two: pp. 214–26

Robbie resumes the narration of the journey to Dunkirk, initially across fields but finally they are drawn to the road. They join the endless column of soldiers and refugees. There are innumerable details of hopelessness and defeat, including the French cavalry unit shooting all its horses ceremonially — 'this enactment of defeat' (p. 219).

There is an incident with a major who wants the stragglers to make a (pointless) assault on a copse; the column is strafed by an ME 109, but Robbie warns them in time to take cover. The major resumes his plan, but is deceived into thinking Robbie is an officer and they move on.

References and allusions

p. 218, HLI men. The Highland Light Infantry, a Scottish infantry regiment.

p. 219: a hexameter. Five iambs and an anapaest. Robbie likens the rhythm of their march to the poetic rhythms he has studied. A hexameter is a line with six stresses; the iamb has two syllables, the second stressed; the anapaest has three syllables, the last stressed.

p. 220, the Buffs. The county regiment of West Kent, which was the local regiment for the Tallises. The name derives from the buff-coloured breeches originally worn by the regiment.

p. 223, RAMC. The Royal Army Medical Corps.

p. 223, ME109. The Messerschmitt 109 was one of the finest fighter planes of the early part of the war. They were used extensively to strafe refugees and the Dunkirk beaches.

Two: pp. 226–34

As he walks on towards Dunkirk, Robbie's thoughts are on the possibility, tantalisingly offered in Cee's last letter, of being cleared and of restarting his life. He thinks of Briony, and tries to understand: 'Yes, she was just a child. But not every child sends a man to prison with a lie' (p. 228).

He recalls the events of June 1932, when Briony was ten, and he had taken her for a swimming lesson in the river: how she had jumped in so that he would have to jump in, fully clothed, to save her. He was angry, but she revealed that it was a test, and she announced that she 'loved' him. There had been no follow-up, but perhaps that had remained in her mind: 'She was the sort of girl who lived in her thoughts' (p. 233). And the meeting on the bridge that fateful evening — why had Briony been there? To intercept him? And was it the betrayal of her love for him that had led to the extremeness of her response?

Two: pp. 234–46

Back on the road, a group of Stukas appears; Robbie runs off into the field, trying to rescue a mother and her son, but she is stubborn and he finally leaves them. They disappear under the next bomb — 'That was why he had to leave them' (p. 238). Although he keeps leaving Nettle and Mace, they keep finding him; and they have an Amo bar. As they arrive at the canal bridge, they see more scenes of defeat — everywhere, soldiers are destroying equipment. The Coldstream Guards are holding the bridge with impressive military discipline, and selecting men to join the defence. At Mace's urging (p. 244), Robbie develops a limp and they support him over the canal bridge.

References and allusions

p. 234, Maginot. The French had based their defence against attack by the Germans upon the Maginot Line, a stupendously expensive line of fortifications that ran from the Dutch border to Switzerland. In the event the Germans simply bypassed the Maginot Line by attacking through Belgium, and the French abandoned it without a fight.

p. 234, the *poilus.* The French infantry soldiers.

p. 235, the rising howl. The sound of attacking Stukas (see note to p. 200).

p. 239, the Green Howards. An infantry regiment from Yorkshire.

p. 240, Welsh Guards. The Guards are the elite infantry of the British army.

p. 242, *In the deserts of the heart / Let the healing fountain start.* A line from W. H. Auden's poem 'In Memory of W. B. Yeats'.

p. 243, NAAFI. The Navy, Army and Air Force Institute — an organisation that provided relaxation for military personnel and sold essential items such as cigarettes — hence the interest in the NAAFI 'dump'.

p. 243, Coldstream Guards. There are two regiments of English Guards, the Coldstreams and the Grenadiers. Coldstream is a town on the river Tweed between England and Scotland.

Two: pp. 246–65

As they arrive in Dunkirk, so Robbie's clarity of thought begins to deteriorate. After surveying the chaos on the beach ('there was a rout, and this was its terminus', p. 247), they go to a bar, but all the drink has long gone. They see a hapless RAF man assaulted by a mob of angry soldiers, in danger of being killed. While Robbie tries to work out what to do, Mace bursts through and carries the man out — allegedly to drown him — but spirits him away while Robbie and Nettle block the door. Night is falling, and 'the RAF man was forgotten' (p. 254). Robbie and Nettle rescue a pig for a gypsy woman, who rewards them with water, wine and food. Night falls. They find a cellar in which to lie down and surreptitiously eat. Robbie slips into delirium, obsessed with the idea that he must go back and bury the boy in the tree with whom this section started (which parallels the idea that he can go back and make atonement for everywhere that he went wrong before). He is waking the others, deliriously shouting 'no'; he goes back to the moment of his arrest, when Cecilia had come out to the car and had said 'I'll wait for you. Come back' (p. 265). Nettle reveals that they will march to a boat at seven. 'I promise, you won't hear another word from me,' Robbie says prophetically (p. 265).

Note that the end of this section is left hanging: the reader can reasonably presume that Robbie got onto a boat the following morning, or the sensitive reader may have spotted the indications that he was actually seriously ill.

Note also the resolution of the motif of this section, with Cecilia's oft-quoted words being finally placed in their original context. This has become a kind of mantra for Robbie; it is what has kept him going.

References and allusions

p. 250, Mile End Road and Sauchiehall Street. The Mile End Road is in the East End of London; Sauchiehall Street is in Glasgow.

p. 262, *Oh, when I was in love with you, Then I was clean and brave.* A poem by A. E. Housman (1859–1936), from *A Shropshire Lad*. The following lines, however, are not encouraging:

> Oh, when I was in love with you
>   Then I was clean and brave,

And miles around the wonder grew
　　How well did I behave.

And now the fancy passes by
　　And nothing will remain,
　　And miles around they'll say that I
　　Am quite myself again.

Part Three: voice of Briony throughout

There are no numbered sections.

Three: pp. 269–77

Briony is a student nurse ('probationer') in a London hospital (she reveals in the postscript that it is St Thomas's Hospital in Lambeth Palace Road, Westminster), across the river from Parliament, in fear of Sister Marjorie Drummond. (Susan Langland commits the unforgivable error of telling a patient her *Christian* name.) It is spring 1940; the hospital is being emptied of patients and prepared for bombing and casualties. Fiona (Lola look-alike) is her only friend. She could, she reflects, have gone to Girton: 'She could have been at her sister's college, rather than her sister's hospital' (p. 275).

References and allusions

p. 270, La Coupole. A famous restaurant in Paris, although there is no evidence that Briony had ever been there.

p. 273, as if they were new girls at Roedean. We were told earlier that Cecilia went to Roedean (see note to p. 52); it may be presumed that Briony did likewise.

Three: pp. 277–82

At the end of the day, Briony reflects; she tells her mother as little as possible, but hears about the evacuees, the breaking of the Triton and of the vase. She keeps a diary, but the entries 'increasingly shaded off into fantasy' (p. 280); 'She was under no obligation to the truth' (p. 280). While staying for a week with her aunt and uncle in Primrose Hill, she typed out her first 103-page story and submitted it to *Horizon* magazine. She analyses modern literature and her goals (pp. 281–82). She has also written to Cecilia.

References and allusions

p. 281, the new magazine, *Horizon*. *Horizon* magazine was a leading left-wing literary magazine of the period. It was founded and edited by Cyril Connolly and Stephen Spender in 1939 (as briefly referred to by Cecilia on p. 212).

Three: pp. 282–86

It is May 1940. As the news from France worsens, Briony's father writes that Paul Marshall and Lola Quincey are to be married. 'Briony was more than implicated in this union. She had made it possible' (p. 285). They must now be 29 and 20. It brings her back to her crime: 'She was unforgivable' (p. 285).

References and allusions
p. 284, Holy Trinity, Clapham Common. Completed in 1776, the architect was Kenton Couse. An illustration may be found at **www.ideal-homes.org.uk/ lambeth/clapham/holy-trinity-1809.htm**.

Three: pp. 287–315

When all is ready the nurses are given the afternoon off. Briony and Fiona hear a concert in St James's Park; they return to find the first convoy of casualties has arrived. Briony carries one stretcher in with difficulty, then leads a group of walking wounded to a ward. She is confused in the face of reality. She cleans a man's leg. She works right through the night, including comforting a dying French boy, Luc Cornet, who believes she is the English girl who came to his father's bakery in Millau every day. He dies as she holds him. When she finally goes to bed, she finds a letter from *Horizon* magazine, which will not publish her novella, *Two Figures by a Fountain*, but dignifies it with an extended critique.

Note that this is the crux of the novel, because the story Cyril Connolly refers to, although related to Part 1 of Atonement, *is much more conventional and static and* **clichéd**. *The* Atonement *that we have sounds much more like the fictionalised alternative, with more plot and tension, proposed by 'CC' of Horizon magazine. It is at this point that the reader may begin to presume that what they have been reading is a later version of what Connolly has been commenting upon.*

References and allusions
p. 288, Liddell Hart's Book. Basil Liddell Hart (1895–1970) was the leading British military strategist of the interwar years, and was an early exponent of armoured warfare. He wrote extensively, but Briony is probably referring to *The Defence of Britain*, published in 1939.

p. 291, a rough triage system. A way of prioritising casualties as they arrive at a hospital.

p. 314, Mrs Elizabeth Bowen. Bowen (1899–1973) was an Irish novelist who settled in Oxford and became a friend of Virginia Woolf and Rosamond Lehmann. Her novel *The Heat of the Day* is one of McEwan's sources for *Atonement* (another example of **intertextuality**).

p. 314, *Dusty Answer.* A novel by Rosamond Lehmann (1901–90), which also has some similarities to *Atonement.*

p. 315, CC. Cyril Connolly; see note to p. 281, and original reference on p. 212.

Three: pp. 315–27

Briony settles into a routine in the shadow of an expected German invasion, which led to 'heightened perception' (p. 316). One Saturday morning (only ten days after the St James's interlude, it transpires, p. 328) Briony sets out. As she walks, she thinks back to CC's letter, implying that she had sanitised reality in the novella (p. 320). She again concludes that she lacks backbone. 'Everything she did not wish to confront was also missing from her novella — and was necessary to it' (p. 320).

   She is on her way to Clapham Common for Lola's wedding. In the church are Hermione and Cecil, Pierrot and Jackson, and three members of the Marshall family — only.

   And as she observes the proceedings, it suddenly crystallises in her mind: she remembers Lola's scratches — and Marshall's (see p. 127) — and realises that it was Marshall who had raped Lola by the lake, a continuation of the earlier assault that Lola had implausibly blamed on the twins (pp. 116–17) (and that Emily had heard, p. 69). 'And what luck that was for Lola — barely more than a child, prised open and taken — to marry her rapist' (p. 324). Briony fantasises that she stands up and calls out the impediment — but she remains silent.

   She is seen by the party as they leave, but she does not emerge until they have dispersed.

Note that a number of the extensive quotations from the Church of England marriage service are pointedly ironic.

References and allusions

p. 315, Local Defence Volunteers. The official title of the Home Guard (see p. 322), civilians in uniform who defended important locations in their free time.

p. 322, Home Guards. See note to p. 315.

p. 322, a squat church. Holy Trinity, Clapham Common; see note to p. 284.

p. 324, tulle and organdie. These are fine, see-through fabrics used to make up bridal dresses.

p. 325, All Souls Oxford. All Souls College is unique among Oxford colleges in that it has no undergraduates, and is therefore the most unworldly of all of them.

p. 326, confetti of skittering triplets. A triplet is a group of three musical notes played in the time usually reserved for two; the effect is of sudden acceleration. This is no doubt one of the bright organ pieces regularly played at the end of a wedding.

Three: pp. 328–49

The climax. Briony intends to walk to Balham, to see Cecilia. She arrives at 43 Dudley Villas. She knocks, and Cecilia finally comes down to sit on the stairs and warily talks to her. They have not met for five years. They go up to Cecilia's room and both smoke; Cecilia reveals that old Mr Hardman is dead, without explaining the significance of this. Then, awkwardly, Robbie appears from the bedroom, and goes into the bathroom. Briony notes that, now, the possibility that he had been killed 'would have made no sense' (p. 338). Robbie, very angry that she is there, accuses her. What has led Briony to change her mind? 'Growing up' (p. 342).

Cecilia intervenes to calm Robbie down; he then spells out what Briony has to do. It becomes clear that they both think Danny Hardman did it, and that Mr Hardman was lying to cover him. Briony drops her bombshell about Paul Marshall (who was the same height as Robbie, making the uncertainty over identity — although this is not explicitly said — more plausible, and therefore less malicious). She reveals that she has just come from his wedding to Lola (what a dramatic item to reveal). They walk Briony to Balham tube station, 'which in three months' time would achieve its terrible form of fame in the Blitz' (p. 348). As she descends to the train, she understands what she must do: 'a new draft, an atonement, and she was ready to begin' (p. 349).

The beginning of this section is the point at which the alternative versions of the story diverge: 'she felt the distance widen between her and another self, no less real, who was walking back towards the hospital' (p. 329). This alerts the reader that there may be a difficulty with the veracity of the version that follows. 'BT London 1999' gives away that this is part of the new draft, part of the atonement.

References and allusions

p. 335, gingham. A cheap, patterned, cotton cloth.

p. 335, Housman, Crabbe. English poets. A. E. Housman (1859–1936), see note to p. 82; George Crabbe (1754–1832).

p. 335, stout. A variety of beer.

p. 348, Balham tube station. Many London tube (underground railway) stations were used as public air-raid shelters during the Blitz, the bombing of London. Balham station was hit by bombs on 14 October 1940, and 68 people were killed.

London, 1999 (pp. 353–72): voice of Briony, aged 77

This is an autobiographical first-person narrative by Briony (at last), on her seventy-seventh birthday, 'saying my farewells' to the Imperial War Museum (IWM), 'letting go' (p. 353). She has been diagnosed with 'vascular dementia', and she reveals her old self-obsession has not abated. As she recounts her taxi ride to the IWM she

reflects, and she reveals that she conflated three hospitals in the account in Part Three — 'the least of my offences against veracity' (p. 356). She passes 'Lord and Lady Marshall' (p. 357) as she enters the IWM — highlighting the lottery of chance that determines life and death. Marshall has become celebrated for his work for charity — a kind of atonement? ('Perhaps he's spent a lifetime making amends', p. 357). Inside, the feedback from the colonel of the Buffs suggests that she has attempted to get the military detail correct, and confirms that she has remained 'Miss Tallis' (p. 360). However: 'If I really cared so much about facts, I should have written a different kind of book' (p. 360).

Back at the flat in Regents Park, she reveals that she had a husband, Thierry, who is dead.

She is driven to Tilney's Hotel, the site of Emily's funeral, 25 years before (p. 363) — which is actually their old house. In the evening comes the entertainment: the story comes full circle. *The Trials of Arabella* is finally performed by the great-grandchildren of Pierrot. And, up in Auntie Venus's room, she reflects on the novel, the story of her life, and all is finally revealed.

Note that the 'letters from old Mr Nettle' suggest that Part Two is Briony's recon-struction of Robbie's final days (p. 353).

It must be presumed that this section does not form part of the novel to which it refers (possibly called Atonement, *but Briony never says). It not only reveals key infor-mation about the relationship between the 'events' and the fictionalised version of them, it also says a great deal about the role of the author of fiction (see 'Postmodernism and intertextuality' on pp. 82–87, and also the discussion of Postmodernism in 'Literary context' on pp. 26–28 of this guide).*

References and allusions
p. 356, St Thomas's Hospital. A medieval hospital rebuilt in 1868, a leading London hospital. Florence Nightingale founded a nursing school there in 1871, hence the references to her.

p. 358, Cruella de Vil. The villain of the novel and film *101 Dalmations*; a re-spelling of 'Cruel Devil'; an archetype for a cruel and heartless woman.

p. 361, dévoré shawl. Dévoré is a method that creates a 'burnt-out' effect in a fabric.

p. 362, LSE. The London School of Economics.

p. 362, Westway. An elevated dual-carriageway road leading into west London; it passes through some drab housing developments.

p. 363, Tilney's Hotel. This is a direct reference to Jane Austen's novel *Northanger Abbey*, in which the young and imaginative Catherine Morland invents scandalous events when staying in the home of the Tilney family (see 'Postmodernism and inter-textuality' on pp. 82-87 of this guide, and the novel's **epigraph**).

p. 364, A Vivaldi Season. *The Four Seasons* by Antonio Vivaldi is, alas, widely employed as background music.

Characters

Briony Tallis

Briony is 13 in Part One, where there is extensive analysis of her character, ostensibly by the neutral novelist; once the reader appreciates that these are 'really' the retrospective comments of an older Briony about her younger self, the reader may be more cautious about accepting the version that is presented. The following might be seen as evidence of the need for caution:

- She is precocious, and a fantasist: she refers to 'my younger sister, Briony Tallis the writer' (p. 4), imagining how Leon may come to view her.
- 'She was one of those children possessed by a desire to have the world just so' (p. 4); there is an extended description of her room and orderliness (pp. 4-5): 'a taste for the miniature', 'an orderly spirit', 'a passion for secrets'.
- Cecilia thinks of 'her frenetic vision' (p. 21).

It is important to note that she is significantly younger than her siblings: Leon is 12 years older, Cecilia ten. Was she a 'love-child', an accident? She has been brought up virtually as an only child, with her siblings having left home when she was still very young. Emily, left alone in the house for days on end by Jack, is clearly close to Briony and fond of her. 'Ah, that hot smooth little body she remembered from its infancy, and still not gone from her, not quite yet' (p. 4) gives a hint of how empty Emily's life will be when she loses Briony, perhaps suggesting that she is trying to keep her last daughter from growing up to postpone the inevitable moment of separation. This may in part explain Briony's self-centredness and lack of adequate consideration for others ('Her effective status as an only child', p. 5).

Cecilia's comment, in a letter to Robbie in 1940 in Part Two, provides a useful perspective: 'They chose to believe the evidence of a silly, hysterical little girl. In fact, they encouraged her by giving her no room to turn back. She was a young thirteen, I know' (p. 209). This shifts the blame somewhat from Briony's mischief to the acts of the adults.

Briony is a precocious but immature 13-year-old in Part One. Her desire to protect her elder brother Leon from his endless stream of girlfriends (p. 4) suggests that she is not yet capable of seeing her elder siblings as sexual adults. This failure plays a major part in her actions, because it leads her to conclude that Robbie is a 'maniac' for having a sexual interest in Cecilia when it is, in fact, perfectly normal and reasonable for him to do so. Equally, this prejudice prevents her from considering the possibility that Cecilia was actually a consensual participant in the sexual encounter she interrupts in the library.

Briony does not feature in Part Two, except in the report of her change of heart, but she is again the focus of Part Three. She has learned humility in the intervening years. We do not know at what point she realised that her testimony had been false,

or what it was that brought her to this realisation — was it gradual, or did some particular event trigger it? One of the criticisms of the novel is that so many key parts of the story are simply not told. At some point, Briony decided not to take up the place she had been offered at Girton College, Cambridge, and instead volunteered to train as a nurse. The outbreak of war was imminent or may have already occurred, and no doubt many others took similar decisions. What we know of Briony in 1940 was written by herself years later, so again it is not reliable evidence; but, as told, it seems that she accepts her treatment by Sister Drummond without chafing too much or fighting back.

Part Three differs from Parts One and Two in that, whereas they are more or less 'true' accounts of what happened, Briony admits, in 'London, 1999', that Part Three is largely imaginary, as Robbie was already dead at the time this section is set. However, all but the section dealing with the meeting with Cecilia and Robbie can be taken as 'true', and although Briony is describing herself there is no particular reason to doubt that at least the outlines 'actually happened', i.e. Briony became a nurse, trained at St Thomas's, endured discomforts and witnessed distressing events. It is the meeting that poses the difficulties: in this case we are doubly at the novelist's mercy, both because this is Briony's account, and because we know that the meeting is pure invention on her part. Nevertheless, we can say that, as she presents herself, she seems contrite, prepared to do whatever is needed to make atonement, and has learned to suppress her natural tendency to defend and justify herself. All this is consistent with the portrait of an older and wiser Briony presented in the remainder of Part Three, and, had Robbie survived and had the meeting taken place, it seems not implausible that it might have been something like this.

'London, 1999' is not part of Briony's novel, and its status is unclear — perhaps a personal memoir, or part of a diary — and it throws interesting light on Briony's character. The most surprising aspect of this section is, perhaps, the casual admission that Briony had once had a husband, Thierry (the French name suggests some connection with the episode in Part Three where Briony comforts the dying Frenchman from Millau, and he deliriously describes the visits of an English girl with whom he fell in love). There were no children, as none feature in the subsequent family reunion, but this reference adds to the frustration of the reader about all the parts of the 'story' that have not been included in the novel.

Otherwise, the 77-year-old Briony seems a convincing and rather moving representation of someone who has lived a troubled, but at least in part satisfying, life (she is a respected novelist) and who is tidying up the loose ends of her personal and professional life in the light of the recent diagnosis of inoperable 'vascular dementia' and the inevitable prospect of the decay of her faculties and, ultimately, extinction. The reader has 'known' Briony since she was 13, and can probably now forgive her childish mistakes; it is sad and sobering to contemplate such a fate for such an intelligent person. She seems, as all elderly people do, rather self-centred

and fastidious, settled into well-worn routines and slightly self-satisfied. It is instructive that the elder Briony sums up her younger self as 'that busy, priggish, conceited little girl' (p. 367).

Briony seems to change significantly between 1935 and 1999, although the reader has to be on guard given that we see the child of 1935 through the eyes and pen of the adult of 1999. It is perhaps unfair to compare a spoilt and immature 13-year-old with a 77-year-old who has just received news of a distressing disease. Nevertheless, it could also be argued that Briony, as presented by herself, has moved from a self-centred and interfering child, through a young adulthood tortured by justified guilt and regret, to an old age that is more like her childhood. Her need for atonement has matured from the raw, urgent need of 1940 into something much more intellectual (even, perhaps, self-indulgent) by the end of her life. When she asks 'how can a novelist achieve atonement' (p. 371), she is accepting that events took matters out of her hands. No matter how guilty she was and felt, she was not able to perform the acts of atonement described in Part Three, and only a fictionalisation of the whole story remains within her power. This cannot benefit Robbie or Cecilia; and she admits, finally, 'The attempt was all' (p. 371).

We are twice told of the earlier incident in which Briony declared her childish love for Robbie and tested his loyalty cruelly by throwing herself into the river and forcing him to save her. This reminds us of the intimate role of Robbie in the life of the family, and throws some light upon the events of the novel. In Robbie's retelling of the incident, on pp. 229–32, it was a key 'to understand this child's mind' (p. 229). He went up to Cambridge afterwards and did not see her for many months; he had assumed the incident forgotten, that Briony had got over it. But had she? Or was she motivated, among many other things, by jealousy in her denunciation of him? Jealousy of an elder sister who did everything first, including going to Cambridge, and had now taken away the man Briony thought she 'loved'? This would make some sense; but Briony's version (p. 342) is different:

> ...there came back to her from years ago, when she was ten or eleven, the memory of a passion she'd had for him, a real crush that had lasted days. Then she confessed it to him one morning in the garden and immediately forgot about it.

This would be at the very least disingenuous, in the light of Robbie's detailed account; but as both these accounts were actually written by Briony, clearly something more complex is afoot; perhaps she wants to raise the possibility that she *did* have wounded residual feelings for Robbie in 1935, even if she subsequently wanted to dismiss or deny them.

In an early draft of *Atonement* McEwan included a brief biography of Briony of the sort that generally appears on the jacket of a novel. He wrote:

> About the author: Briony Tallis was born in Surrey in 1922, the daughter of a senior civil servant. She attended Roedean School, and in 1940 trained to

become a nurse. Her wartime nursing experience provided the material for her first novel, *Alice Riding*, published in 1948 and winner of that year's Fitzrovia Prize for fiction. Her second novel, *Soho Solstice*, was praised by Elizabeth Bowen as 'a dark gem of psychological acuity', while Graham Greene described her as 'one of the more interesting talents to have emerged since the war'. Other novels and short-story collections consolidated her reputation during the fifties. In 1962 she published *A Barn in Steventon*, a study of domestic theatricals in Jane Austen's childhood. Tallis's sixth novel, *The Ducking Stool*, was a best-seller in 1965 and was made into a successful film starring Julie Christie. Thereafter, Briony Tallis's reputation went into a decline, until the Virago imprint made her work available to a younger generation in the late seventies. She died in July 2001. (Quoted in Finney: see 'Further study' on p. 104 of this guide.)

Robbie Turner

Robbie is the other character who is granted a substantial proportion of the narrative voice, throughout Part Two and for sections of Part One. The impression of Robbie formed from reading Part One lacks clear focus. Cecilia's view of him is confused for much of this section, and once she understands her complex feelings for him, events overtake her. Briony's voice, in which he is typecast as a 'maniac', dominates the section. When we hear Robbie's own viewpoint, in Chapter 8, he comes across as intelligent and very well read (unlike Cecilia, who does not). His frustration with the position of dependence in which he finds himself is understandable: he is able to pursue his academic ambitions, which are far more deserving than Cecilia's (who is a mere dilettante), only because of the charity of Jack Tallis. There is a suspicion that he has not received this charity because he merits it (although his First Class degree amply confirms that he does) but simply as a kind of assuaging of guilt by Jack (although we do not know what for): 'But really, he was a hobby of Jack's, living proof of some levelling principle he had pursued through the years' (p. 151). This hints at a sympathy with socialism for which there is no other evidence; but as we never actually see Jack Tallis, the reader is unable to investigate this suggestion further.

Cecilia's views of him, especially at the time of the fountain incident, are decidedly ungenerous, emphasising his tendency to be a victim to fads: 'his Communist Party time — another abandoned fad, along with his ambitions in anthropology, and the planned hike from Calais to Istanbul' (p. 22). The reader may see these, along with his new-found interest in medicine, as evidence of the width of interests of an intelligent young man constrained by his circumstances. Alternatively, they may indicate that he is a fantasist with an insecure grip on reality. Note that even Emily thinks of Robbie as having 'something manic and glazed in his look' (p. 151).

The other issue concerns his sexual appetites. We learn, on p. 204, that he had been diagnosed as 'morbidly over-sexed'. The modern reader is unlikely to find this convincing, although we have little evidence, and it might be thought that the phrase in his fatal letter, 'In my thoughts I make love to you all day long' (p. 86) suggests a greater level of desire than is usual. However, allowing for literary hyperbole, the fact that he is a frustrated 23-year-old virgin in love and that the addendum was never intended to be read, he seems pretty normal.

By the time we see him in Part Two, Robbie has changed significantly. He has grown up considerably, and his bitterness at the unfairness of the treatment that has robbed him of the best years of his life has become somewhat muted in the circumstances in which he finds himself — although occasional flashes can be seen. His experiences in prison mean that, uniquely, he finds life in the army, even when under training, not particularly uncomfortable. He has matured, and now seems much more focused than the 23-year-old who could never settle to anything. He has developed natural leadership qualities ('He acted like an officer, but he didn't even have a single stripe', p. 193), which may well have always been latent (is his dogged pursuit and recovery of the twins evidence of this?). His attitude to the army is peculiarly ambiguous, as it was responsible for his early release from prison (we never discover what his sentence actually was). It is therefore especially cruel that the military situation in France in 1940 gave him no opportunity to make use of his leadership skills in a useful context. Instead, they are employed in the attempt to escape and return to Cecilia, a reunion that seems to have been doomed from the start. Nevertheless, despite the way in which society has treated him, and his experiences of defeat and retreat, his humanity is not diminished. He is moved by the sight of the dead boy's leg in the tree (p. 192), he risks his life attempting to save the woman and her son (pp. 235–8), and is horrified by the mob's response to the plight of the RAF man at Bray-les-Dunes (although it is Mace who takes the initiative and saves him). He is fixated upon getting back to see Cecilia again; and although he half fears that this is a fantasy, her letters are enough to keep him going. This is a far cry from the Robbie we saw, and whom Cecilia was contemptuous of, in Part One, constantly flitting from one enthusiasm to another.

We see Robbie briefly again in Part Three, an episode we know to be entirely the product of Briony's imagination. Robbie seems distracted when he appears in Cecilia's flat. We are not told how long he has been there, or how severe his wound turned out to be, but we are told that he has to report back to his unit that evening. (We should not forget that at this stage in the summer of 1940 it was expected that a German invasion was imminent and that those evacuated from Dunkirk would soon be back in action.) During the conversation he becomes animated, then angry, and has to be restrained by Cecilia. Nevertheless, he allows her to calm him down and discusses flatly with Briony what needs to be done. There is an air of fatigue about him. At this point the layers of authorship need to be taken into account. McEwan no doubt has a clear and consistent Robbie in mind, and 'lends' this to Briony for her to make her fictionalised portrait of this imaginary encounter plausible — which it is.

Briony is a novelist but her life-novel is based, she claims, on events which actually happened to her. Given that she never spoke to Robbie after 1935, and probably never spoke to Cecilia again either (she says in 'London, 1999' that she turned back after Lola's wedding, and only three months later Cecilia was killed), the reader is entitled to ask how 'reliable' her presentation of Robbie, his character and his inner life is. This is a fiction within a fiction, and is the heart of the conundrum of the novel. Given that all the characters and events are inventions by McEwan, including Briony, it seems rather quaint to ask whether Briony's depictions of McEwan's creations are convincing or not. Similarly, the issue of when and where Robbie 'died' requires a complex conception of the reader's belief (or suspension of disbelief) in the novelist's fictional world. The representation is as McEwan intended it. It is also as Briony intended it, given that the entire novel is presented as hers. It is true by definition that her presentation is 'consistent', in that there is no external evidence or criterion to which appeal could be made. A **Postmodernist** author denies the reader the satisfaction of thinking that they will be told 'what happened' to the characters in whose reality they have consented to believe (see 'Postmodernism and intertextuality' on pp. 82–87 of this guide).

Cecilia Tallis

Briony clearly knew Cecilia much better than she ever knew Robbie, but it should not be forgotten that Cecilia is 10 years older than Briony and left for university when Briony was barely 10. It must be borne in mind that all the descriptions of Cecilia in Part One, including those sections purporting to be from her viewpoint, were in fact written by Briony many years later with the benefit of hindsight. This may cause the reader to be cautious. Briony needs to make these episodes psychologically convincing, and the reader may not feel there is anything out of place in the strangely listless attitudes displayed by Cecilia in the earlier chapters of Part One. (The sensitive reader may recognise echoes of the listlessness depicted in the equally stifling summer of *The Go-Between*, one of the key texts to which *Atonement* can be compared.)

Nevertheless, the reader probably feels that Cecilia is rather a spoilt child; she has come down from Cambridge, not especially sheepish about having achieved only a Third Class degree (and therefore having been shamed by Robbie's First, a dimension that cannot be overestimated; see 'Social class' on pp. 64–68 of this guide), and seems devoid of any sense of urgency about selecting something constructive to do with her life. Her room is described, tellingly, as 'a stew of unclosed books, unfolded clothes, unmade bed, unemptied ashtrays' (pp. 4–5; note the stylistic effect of this succession of negative prefixes).

For all her enthusiasm for her social life at Cambridge, it does not seem to have included any men; none are named or mentioned, she has no current boyfriend, and it is revealed in Chapter 11 that not only is she still a virgin, but 'she had no experience at all' (p. 136). She also seems, at the age of 23 and about to go out into the world, indifferent to this situation. Her stated reason for spending an empty summer at home is: 'she had hung about the house all summer, encouraged by a vague notion she was re-establishing an important connection with her family' (p. 103). 'There was desperation in all she said, an emptiness at its core' (p. 109), and the reader must speculate as to which of many possible emptinesses this is.

There are repeated references in Part One to the fact that Cecilia smokes; this is another class issue. It was considered normal for a gentleman to smoke; indeed, most country houses had a smoking room, to which the gentlemen would withdraw after a meal while the women withdrew to the [with]drawing room. It was not considered polite for a woman to smoke (although this did not apply to working-class women). In the 1930s, however, it was considered 'Bohemian' (arty, lefty, trendy) for middle-class women to smoke. Cecilia presumably took it up at Cambridge, but her mother strongly disapproves. That she smokes so brazenly is a rather feeble gesture of independence (given how dependent she really is, and how devoid of any real plans for her future). Emily disapproves, but does not have the energy or passion to do anything about it. Smoking is of course addictive, and Cecilia's enslavement to it is perhaps evidence of a weak and suggestible personality.

There are repeated references to Cecilia in Part Two (through Robbie's eyes), and there is a substantial meeting in Part Three, in which it is clear that she has changed since Part One. Cecilia seems to have grown up and to have become resigned to her fate. Perhaps it is a lack of imagination that leads her to remain loyal to Robbie (there is not much evidence of romanticism in her nature; much more in his), and we are given no indication of how she passed the four years between the court case and the outbreak of war, that led her to take up nursing. We know she left home and cut herself off from her family (a petulant or romantic gesture?). She had persuaded herself that she was in love with Robbie, but on the flimsiest of evidence and with no opportunity to establish a real basis for it except his lustful and premature attempt to have sex with her in the library. It is hard to avoid the conclusion that she is rather immature and headstrong to react in this way. Robbie is rightly worried about how matters will be between them when they finally meet, and the fantasy **epistolary** relationship of the prison years has to be measured against reality. We do not know whether she was equally concerned that the whole thing might have been based on an illusion. In the imagined meeting with Briony in Part Three, which Briony of course has invented, Cecilia is an interesting mixture of anger and realism. 'Don't worry', Cecilia says, 'I won't ever forgive you' (p. 337). But she calms Robbie down in order to arrive at a sensible plan.

Lola Quincey

The name 'Lola' is reminiscent of Lolita, the **eponymous** central character of Vladimir Nabokov's novel about a 'nymphet' — a girl who allows herself to be seduced by an older man. Although Lola is, in one sense, at the heart of the novel's

plot, she is rarely at the centre of the stage. Chapter 5 of Part One appears to be told from her perspective, but otherwise her fleeting appearances are seen through the eyes of others. Arguably, she is at least as responsible as Briony for Robbie's fate.

It is difficult to form a clear view of Lola's character. This may be because all the glimpses of her derive from Briony, who may either find her unaccountable, or may be too angry with her to be able to do her justice. Although it is clear that Briony appreciates that Lola is on the brink of womanhood, in a way that Briony is not, she does not give any very penetrating insights into her character. 'All three were ginger-haired and freckled' (p. 9) is a rather dismissive view of her appearance, in contrast to Paul Marshall's view: she was 'almost a young woman, poised and imperious, quite the little pre-Raphaelite princess' (p. 60). Crucially, we are never told what happened between her and Marshall in the playroom in the afternoon; we must construct it from the 'little squeal of laughter abruptly smothered' (p. 69) overheard by Emily, and the 'two-inch scratch' (p. 127) seen by Robbie by the time that dinner starts. Presumably Lola enjoyed the attention until Marshall went too far and she fought him off. How the 'rape' scene came about is a mystery, as is what was going through Lola's mind behind her equivocal utterances while she desperately constructed a way to exculpate herself after what had just happened. All we know is that five years later she had decided to throw in her lot with Marshall, and we discover in 'London, 1999' that she has done very nicely out of it. Whether she was ever troubled by her conscience is not recorded.

Paul Marshall

Marshall enjoys a similar status to Lola; he is the rapist of an under-age girl. The injustice of his elevation to a Lord reflects his wealth more than his character. We see three rather impressionistic glimpses of him in the novel. In Chapter 4 of Part One, as he drones on about the Amo bar, Cecilia allows herself to fantasise about having a relationship with such a rich man, but the picture she paints is hardly flattering: 'a man so nearly handsome, so hugely rich, so unfathomably stupid. He would fill her with his big-faced children, all of them loud, bone-headed boys' (p. 50). Lola's view, although more ambivalent, is little better: 'It was a cruel face, but his manner was pleasant, and this was an attractive combination, Lola thought' (p. 58). What is quickly clear is that if anyone in the novel is 'morbidly over-sexed' (p. 204), it is Marshall, not Robbie (who did nothing at all when Cecilia stripped to her underwear in his company). The brief section written from Marshall's perspective in Chapter 5 (p. 60) reveals him as sexually aroused by the thought of his four younger sisters 'touching and pulling at his clothes'. He then goes into the playroom, having stood for some time at the door observing (p. 58), and presumably doing so because he fancied getting to know the 15-year-old he saw. His evaluation of her (p. 60) certainly makes her sound more like a potential lover than a child.

The wedding of Marshall and Lola in Part Three gives Briony the opportunity to work out, finally, what really happened on that fateful day in 1935; but other than

the fact that he married Lola five years later (we do not know what had happened in the intervening years), we learn nothing more about him. Perhaps the fact that it is a private ceremony (despite his wealth) suggests some degree of embarrassment about the whole thing.

By 'London, 1999', Lord and Lady Marshall have come a long way and have become pillars of society. The fact that the black Jaguar, first seen at the wedding, has been retained as something of a trademark suggests perhaps some sentimental attachment to the past. Marshall poses for the photographers and seems generally smug, but this hardly throws any light on his character. Nevertheless, the glimpses of Part One are probably sufficient for us to be convinced of the plausibility of his role in the events of that day as they are finally revealed.

Leon

The name 'Leon' is generally thought to be Jewish, although there is no suggestion that the Tallis family is of Jewish origin. It may echo 'Leo' in *The Go-Between*, although there is no similarity in their roles. Although, as Briony's elder brother, he might be expected to have an iconic status, there is little evidence of this in Part One. Leon hardly appears in the remainder of the novel until he is seen in his wheelchair at the family reunion in 'London, 1999', and it is reasonable to ask why he exists at all. Leon is a remarkably shadowy character. His vagueness lends strength to a suspicion that the whole Tallis family is rather lacking in something; he lacks vigour, commitment and purpose. Cecilia, too, seems to have been unmotivated at Cambridge, and has just lazed around the house since coming down, listlessly and without any plans for her future.

Although Briony waits avidly for her brother's return, and wrote the play to impress him, she has remarkably little to do with him once he arrives. The tone is set by Emily in Chapter 6, who sees him as 'the humblest soul in a private bank, and living for the weekends and his rowing eight' (p. 64); he is 'Too handsome, too popular, no sting of unhappiness and ambition' (p. 64). Cecilia's view is similar; she sees him as having 'the pure gift of avoiding responsibility' (p. 102). To her mind, 'Leon had always floated free' (p. 103); 'His blandness was perfectly tolerable, even soothing' (p. 108); 'The agreeable nullity of Leon's life was a polished artefact' (p. 109).

Leon's principal role in the plot could be seen as bringing Marshall to the house (ironically, Emily speculates that 'One day he might bring home a friend for Cecilia to marry' (p. 64); the friend ends up marrying Lola, and Cecilia turns out not to need any help in finding a partner).

Emily Tallis

Emily Tallis is examined in some depth in Part One, although scarcely thereafter (note that two of the chapters, 6 and 12, are presented through her eyes). The use of her first name by her children is rather surprising in the 1930s; it suggests that

her parental authority role is limited. She is effectively seen as an invalid, and can therefore be excused her dereliction of parental duties. There is some suspicion that her invalid status is self-inflicted (she avoids migraine by an elaborate regime of withdrawal to her room). The children are in a sense complicit in this, especially Cecilia, in that they have taken on many of her duties. 'Her mother had always lived in an invalid's shadow land' (p. 103).

Emily is not directly responsible for anything that happens. Her responsibility arguably goes back a long way — to Briony's spoilt nature, or her feverish imagination — but these are mere preconditions for the events of June 1935. She is an example of a woman whose potential has been wasted; she was not allowed to go to university, unlike her children, but she is clearly sensitive. With her heightened sense of hearing, she lies in her darkened room and has developed 'a tentacular awareness that reached out from the dimness and moved through the house, unseen and all-knowing… The less she was able to do, the more she was aware' (p. 66). But the truth of the suddenly changed relationship between Cecilia and Robbie eluded her, so that she was happy to go along with the false accusation against Robbie. Partly, we know, this derives from resentment at Jack wasting their money on him, partly from resentment at Robbie's First as compared with Cecilia's Third, and probably underlying all of it a snobbish prejudice against her daughter being compromised by the son of their cleaner.

Jack Tallis

This character is notable principally by his absence; Jack Tallis does not appear as the voice in any part of the novel. One telephone conversation is recounted in Chapter 12, from Emily's point of view; the writer's pointed reference to him as 'the senior Civil Servant' (p. 154) emphasises how far the job has taken him over, and how far he is from being an effective member of the family. He reacts firmly and with accustomed authority when he hears of the absence of the twins; but when he is informed by Leon of the graver crime, we do not hear his reaction. It does not surprise the reader that a car breakdown prevents him from arriving in time to play any part in the drama, and he is therefore never actually seen in the novel. Nor is he mentioned later when Emily's death is reported, but we are told (p. 355) that he remarried, presumably after her death.

The whole novel is characterised by an absence of positive male figures. The father of the Tallis children is absent; Robbie's father is permanently absent; Leon is a lightweight, Marshall is cynical and corrupt. Robbie is the only strong male, and circumstances conspire to bring him down. Perhaps an unrecognised part of Briony's feelings towards Robbie (love, jealousy, hatred) is a reaction to his usurpation of the roles that should be played by her absent father and feeble brother.

The relationship between Jack and Emily Tallis is a strange one, even for the 1930s. Partly this is a result of the extraordinary feebleness of Emily. A self-declared

invalid who has abdicated her role as mother (except for enjoying the last few moments in which she can mother Briony before she slips away into adolescence), she is resigned to her husband's absence and presumed infidelity to a degree which is almost pathological. When Jack phones (as she knew he would) to go through the daily charade of giving an excuse for his not returning home that night, Emily's response (as reconstructed retrospectively by Briony, of course) is 'she did not mind, for he would be back at the weekend, and one day he would be home for ever and not an unkind word would be spoken' (p. 153). The writer observes 'The exchange held a trace of affection, and its familiarity was comfort.'

Danny Hardman

'Danny' is a common working-class name, but it may also echo the Bible story of Daniel in the lion's den. 'Hardman' is a striking name! Danny is not really a character in the novel; he is never heard to speak. He does play an important role, however, because he is carefully built up as a possible rapist of Lola: 'She had noticed him hanging around the children lately. Perhaps he was interested in Lola. He was sixteen, and certainly no boy' (p. 48). Otherwise he is not a presence, and it comes as something of a surprise when we discover, in Part Two, Cecilia's conviction that he must have been the rapist — another example of class prejudice. It is ironic in Cecilia's case that she replaces the unfair accusation against one young working-class male with that against another, never for a moment suspecting the true villain. 'When Hardman decided to cover for Danny' (p. 209) she writes, thereby maligning the innocent father along with the son. It is left to Briony to rehabilitate Danny's character in Part Three (p. 346).

War and peace

The summer of 1935 was an oasis of peace sandwiched between two wars. Briony's Uncle Clem was killed in France during the Great War, and the vase that he had been given during the conflict plays a key part in the events. It seems likely that Robbie's absent father was also killed during the war. The shadow of a new war already hangs over this idyllic summer: Briony's father is held up in London working on endless contingency plans for the coming hostilities, whereas, by contrast, guest Paul Marshall is looking forward to making a fortune by selling his new 'Amo' bars to thousands of called-up soldiers. The name ironically links war and love: 'amo' is Latin for 'I love', as all prep school boys know, but also echoes 'ammo' (ammunition). Equally ironically, at the end of the novel Lord and Lady Marshall are seen at the Imperial War Museum — a monument to the war that made their fortune.

It is an interesting question whether the wartime setting is essential to the novel's success. Part One is set in a time of peace, and although war is distantly on

the horizon it does not influence the events in any way. The remainder of the novel, though, would have been unrecognisably different. Although the wrongful accusation against Robbie would have caused distress at any time, it is given added poignancy by the intervention of war. It seems clear that Cecilia remained faithful to Robbie, so although we are (curiously) never told the length of his sentence for the crime he did not commit, it is reasonable to suppose that he would have come out sooner or later and Cecilia would have been waiting for him. If Briony had been able to go through with her intention of withdrawing her testimony, Robbie might have been released relatively soon, and he and Cecilia either would or would not have established a successful relationship. This would have been a very different novel, on a less heroic scale and with less resonance. In the novel as we have it, the onset of war allowed Robbie to cut short his sentence, but at the price of a more cruel one — he met Cecilia once more and then died before he could see her again. Briony's attempts at making useful atonement are thwarted by the historical context, and the characters all become pawns in the face of larger historical forces.

The war makes the entire remainder of the novel possible. Robbie would not have joined the army and could not have experienced the events of Part Two without it. Neither Cecilia nor Briony would conceivably have become nurses other than in wartime, so Part Three could not exist either. Without the war, Briony would not have been forced to find atonement through her fiction. It is also the case that the wartime setting changes reader expectations: in war it is expected that one or more characters will become a victim of the hostilities, and there is a literary tradition that characters in war carry over into combat problems in their personal lives. The transition to war also allows Robbie's character to be filled out: he proves resourceful and reliable in extreme circumstances, and has an opportunity to demonstrate his leadership potential, which would probably not have arisen in peacetime.

It is clear from 'London, 1999' that Briony went to considerable lengths to ensure that the military details of the retreat to Dunkirk depicted in Part Two were accurate. There is a significant amount of military jargon; a number of individual regiments are identified (e.g. the Buffs, the HLI, the West Kents) as well as some arms of service (RA, RAMC) and other abbreviations (BEF, NAAFI). Stukas and ME109s are virtually the only items of military kit individually identified. A military historian might well find it a bit thin (i.e. a convincing version of what a novelist such as Briony might construct from a museum). McEwan, as the son of an army major, would have had no difficulty in making this section more convincing had he chosen to do so. The effect is to persuade the reader of the naturalistic nature of this section; it is seen from Robbie's perspective, and since he joined up these military details had become the setting of his life. It was important for Briony that this illusion should be successfully maintained, hence the effort she made.

Many people have been given the impression that Dunkirk was a triumph for the British, but in reality the defeat of the BEF in France in 1940 was a shocking military

defeat (see the section on 'Dunkirk and the fall of France' on pp. 22–24 of this guide). The extraction of so many of the soldiers from Dunkirk was a remarkable achievement, attributable as much to the faltering German High Command as to the 'pluck' of the sailors of the armada of small boats that made the hazardous Channel crossing to bring the soldiers back. Winston Churchill, the British prime minister, was clear that a withdrawal was not a victory, and the loss of all the fighting equipment of the British army was a disaster that could not have been overcome before the invading German army arrived. Only the success of the Royal Air Force in deterring a German invasion by the Battle of Britain saved the country from certain defeat. *Atonement* gives a brutally honest account of the disintegration of the army in the undisciplined retreat to the coast; only elite units, such as the Guards, and those with high-quality officers, remained effective. For a long time, all this was glossed over in Britain. McEwan writes feelingly of this retreat, as his father was involved in it; he explained in an interview for the *San Francisco Chronicle*:

> Well, the whole of the British army was at Dunkirk. My father was a motorbike dispatch rider. He was injured by shrapnel in the legs and this other man was wounded in the arms. Between them, they worked the controls of the Harley Davidson. I grew up with his Dunkirk stories. I found from contemporary accounts the frustration of ordinary soldiers that they didn't see enough air cover. Some journalist here disputed that, but all of these old colonels and the like have written in saying it was true. Certainly from the soldiers' point of view, they were sitting ducks.
>
> (From www.sfgate.com/cgi-bin/article.cgi?file=/chronicle/archive/2002/03/10/ RV51718.DTL)

The setting of Part Three is coloured by the awareness of war in the background, and the activity in the hospital is very different to what it would be in peacetime. There is a contrast between the endless, meticulous preparations, and the semi-chaos once the convoy of casualties arrives. In peacetime patients either arrive in a steady trickle, and are dealt with in a routine way, or they come as the result of a major incident, in which case there is no opportunity to prepare. The lengthy period of waiting (echoing the 'phoney war' period of many months following the declaration of war in September 1939, when, for Britain at least, very little happened) allows the hospital to be emptied of patients in readiness for a sudden influx which, the old-timers know, will be horrific. When it comes, its scale and horror are seen through Briony's eyes, and we share her reactions to it. It involves physical and mental trauma on a scale with which she is completely unfamiliar.

The key characters in the novel are profoundly affected by the advent and experience of war. Robbie has changed the most, but how much of this is attribut-able to the experience of trial, conviction and prison is open to question. He seems to have been a much more mature person, by his own account (albeit actually Briony's, of course), by the time of his one meeting with Cecilia before he is posted

to France. His experience of the army and of defeat and retreat have made him very focused. His natural leadership qualities have emerged: 'He acted like an officer, but he didn't even have a single stripe' (p. 193), and despite what he has experienced and witnessed his humanity is undiminished. He is determined to see Cecilia again; and although he half fears that this is a fantasy, her letters are enough to keep him going. This is a far cry from the Robbie we saw, and of whom Cecilia was contemptuous, in Part One, constantly flitting from one enthusiasm to another. He summarises the experience of war: 'First his own life ruined, then everybody else's' (p. 217).

Cecilia appears to have undergone a similar transformation. In Part One she was listless, lacking in ambition and without any plans for her future. No doubt the discovery of Robbie's love, and her reciprocation of it, explains her strange mood at that time, and the subsequent experience of his trial and conviction will have contributed to her growing up. The Cecilia whom Briony fictitiously meets in Part Three is an adult, who has made her choice to become a nurse for the duration of the war, although it is unlikely that this would have satisfied her once hostilities were over. It is apparent from her dealings with Briony that she has moved beyond the blind anger of the earlier years, and she calms Robbie down and encourages him to look constructively to the future.

Briony has grown from an immature, spoilt 13-year-old to an adult by Part Three, and the experience of discovering the awful truth about what she has done no doubt contributed as much as anything else to her changed attitude. She is now humble and prepared to accept humiliation, which she knows she deserves. The choice of nursing, involving as it does giving up the place at Girton, Cambridge, for which she had worked, is evidence of this, as is her demeanour in general. The war lends urgency to this, and her experiences with the wounded soldiers in the hospital confirm her new, more realistic view of herself.

Sex and relationships

Sex, consensual and otherwise, is at the very heart of this novel. There is very little of it, but what there is is particularly momentous. In very different circumstances, both Cecilia and Lola lose their virginity the same evening, and in each case the issue of consent is contentious. Neither, as far as we can tell, initiated it, but both, as far as we can tell, choose to accept it — sooner or later — as consensual.

The novel starts as a rather innocent account of a childish play being prepared by a group of children, but through a series of stages the reader is prepared for the appearance of explicit sexuality in this rural idyll. Although Briony's play is childish, there is a tradition of licentiousness in amateur theatricals (e.g. in Jane Austen's *Mansfield Park*). The encounter of Robbie and Cecilia by the fountain and Cecila's undressing (Chapter 2) are clearly potentially erotic even if the reader has not detected that these two are unwittingly emotionally engaged with one another. The adult reader may well suspect Paul Marshall's motives when he enters the room of the Quincey children (Chapter 5) and flirts blatantly with Lola. (Note that, although this chapter is supposedly recounted from Lola's viewpoint, there is a short digression that informs us that, in Marshall's eyes, Lola was 'almost a young woman, poised and imperious, quite the little pre-Raphaelite princess', p. 60). The chapter ends with the dismissal of the twins, leaving Lola and Marshall alone. It is Chapter 8, though, that makes the sexual element suddenly (and apparently incongruously) apparent, when Robbie writes his obscene letter to Cecilia. This makes it seem as if it is Robbie who has introduced vulgarity to the seemly atmosphere of the Tallis household, but in reality this is a response to Cecilia's provocative behaviour earlier.

The fountain scene is a key episode in the novel. The publisher's blurb on most editions of *Atonement* refers to Cecilia stripping off and entering the fountain on the hottest day of the year. It is Briony's uncomprehending witnessing of this scene that sets her mind off on the wrong track for the rest of the day. Immersed in romantic fiction of her own and others' creation, she knows nothing about sex, unlike a 13-year-old of today. The act of stripping to underwear — without even telling Robbie to avert his eyes, as would have been expected in polite society — is incontestably erotic as well as provocative, as his later comment about 'a glimpse of the triangular darkness her knickers were supposed to conceal' (p. 79) indicates. Whatever was going through her mind, at least an unconscious desire to parade sexually in front of Robbie must have been part of it — perhaps along with a snobbish desire to show off her social superiority in that she did not judge him worthy of being treated as an equal, in front of whom she could not have acted like that.

The action of Part One takes place on one of the hottest days of the summer (as it does in *The Go-Between*). It is a literary commonplace that the so-called 'warm-blooded' Mediterranean peoples are more likely to show their passion than cold-blooded northerners. Equally, though, when exposed to serious heat, the English are thought to lose their inhibitions and behave more like Mediterraneans. Certainly the heat encourages people to reduce or remove their clothing; but they seem also to find their passions and lusts enflamed in some rather primitive way. How else is one to explain the fact that Marshall seduces Lola, and Robbie reveals his love for Cecilia by making love to her, without discussing it or even securing her consent in advance? It is as if the heat ignites lust to such a degree that English men are incapable of withstanding it (perhaps because they are so unused to such a phenomenon).

The first (rejected) letter that Robbie writes to Cecilia seems shockingly explicit and vulgar in the context of what has gone before. The vulgarity is an afterthought, which 'ruins' the carefully constructed letter that Robbie has just typed. But he has just referred to Freud and the *Three Essays on Sexuality* (p. 84), and we are reminded

that he is both a literary scholar and a potential medical student. The reference to Freud also prepares the reader for the eruption of Robbie's subconscious, aroused by the events of the day (we presume he has never seen Cecilia in her underwear before, something of which she must also have been aware when she provoked him by stripping off in front of him). What these words do is to break the spell carefully woven in the previous pages of an innocent summer world (consistent with this part having been written by Briony in her naive 13-year-old **persona**), and bring the reader to confront the reality that Robbie and Cecilia are adults, in their mid-20s, and have already spent three years at university. It prepares us for the adult events that are to follow.

The scene in which Robbie attempts to make love to Cecilia in the library (pp. 130–39) raises key questions about whether this sudden sexual encounter was in fact consensual. We see this scene, though, only as Briony can reconstruct it some years later, now aware of its significance. Although the novel tantalisingly omits everything that happened after Robbie was driven off by the police, we must presume that at some point Cecilia angrily told anyone who would listen that the scene in the library that Briony had witnessed, and that played such an important part in creating the atmosphere in which Robbie could be believed guilty of rape, was one in which she had been a willing participant. Presumably, all that Briony saw was what she describes on pp. 123–24 and interpreted as an attack that Cecilia was attempting to ward off. It seems clear that receipt of Robbie's letter had broken a dam in Cecilia's mind and enabled her to make sense of her strange mood and feelings; but she is still adjusting to the implications of these ideas. What the couple needed was time to discuss them, but matters move very fast in the library. Cecilia wonders what he means when he says 'It wasn't the version I intended to send' (p. 132) — does that mean it is not true? Although the lovemaking has not been discussed or agreed and all happens very suddenly, it is clear that Cecilia becomes a full and willing participant as the action develops. Retrospectively, after she has had time to think, she no doubt judges that it was what she had wanted.

The location of these events can be viewed as significant in a number of ways. Some would view it as a desecration of a place dedicated to quiet study, although others would see the literary precedents for the passion of the young lovers and see it as wholly appropriate. The place also emphasises the **intertextual** quality of their relationship, nurtured as it has been by the study of literature (Robbie reinforces this in Part Two, where he lists celebrated literary lovers).

The 'rape' of Lola (pp. 164–67) is the other crucial event of the novel. The reader finally discovers, in 'London, 1999', what really happened. It is instructive to read this scene again in the light of what is subsequently revealed, for it immediately becomes clear that the scene is a masterpiece of ambiguity. There are three overlaid versions:

- Lola's initial belief that Briony saw Marshall having sex with her, without protest
- Briony's initial belief that the man she has just seen is Robbie

- Lola's increasingly conscious acquiescence in what she comes to realise is a falsehood that will exonerate her, but that serves to confirm Briony's initial mistaken impression

While the reader may doubt that the rapist was Robbie, they are likely to believe the implication that what happened was, indeed, rape, whoever the real perpetrator may have been. It is true that Lola cried out as Briony approached, with 'a high, unpleasant call' (p. 164) but this may well have been surprise at the moment of penetration rather than a cry of protest. Lola's first words are 'I'm sorry,' (p. 165) a curious way to express horror at being violated; she presumably intended to apologise for having allowed Marshall to have his way, or for not taking part in the search for the missing twins, or it may perhaps even be an apology to herself for having succumbed to Marshall's approaches. Then, when Briony says 'I saw him!', Lola simply says 'Yes' (p. 165). They are clearly at cross-purposes, and Lola is terrified of the shame and punishment that will result from the discovery that she has allowed Marshall to have sex with her. There then follow crucial minutes in which Lola agrees that 'it was him', (p.165) although the two girls are referring to different men. When, finally, Briony mentions Robbie's name, Lola refuses to confirm it. Presumably she cannot believe her luck. During the long silences, she is probably constructing the alternative story, which she produces on p. 167, that her eyes were covered and she could not see who it was. What was she doing, supposedly sitting alone on the grass by the temple? No one ever asks, but it enabled a 'classical seduction' to take place.

It has been suggested that the failures of the relationships in the parental generation, or the absence of effective father figures, have affected the attitudes and behaviour of the younger characters in the novel. It could be argued that the attitudes of the younger generation towards sex and relationships may have been coloured by their perceptions of their elders. The Quincey children have come to the Tallis household because of the spectacular break-up of their parents' marriage; the relationship of Jack and Emily Tallis is equally dead, differing only in that they both conspire in the fantasy that Jack stays in his flat in London throughout the week because of the pressures of work. Robbie is also the product of a failed relationship in that his father vanished when he was a child and he was brought up by his mother. In fact, it could be argued that all of the younger generation in the novel have effectively been brought up by single mothers and lack father figures. The abdication of parental responsibility by both Jack (through absence) and Emily Tallis (through illness) is something that is tacitly accepted by all parties: Cecilia has long taken on a parental role ('ultimately the success of the evening would be in Cecilia's care', p. 102). This has forced the children to grow up more quickly than would have been usual in upper-middle-class circles, and to establish more independent roles; their use of their mother's first name reveals the absence of the conventional

restraints of middle-class life of the period. They have all established their own roles and rules; there is no mention of religion, either, and in fact external moral frameworks are notable by their absence. Leon, Cecilia and Briony are all, in the end, rather selfish. We know less about Lola, although the effect of her parents' publicised divorce, at her age, must have left her feeling insecure and eager to grasp at an opportunity for a degree of security. The comments about her parents suggest irresponsibility on their part, which would hardly have constituted a moral role model for the daughter to follow.

The 1930s was an era when contradictory attitudes to sexual morality were common. Society's official position remained conservative; among 'Bohemian' circles, a more relaxed attitude prevailed, which could be a cause of tension for several of the characters. Although there is a fair amount of illicit sexual activity either attempted or carried out during the novel, there is remarkably little evidence of any sense of guilt about it. It could be argued that it is in the family heritage of the Tallises: 'common-law marriages unrecorded in the parish registers' (p. 21) suggests a degree of sexual licentiousness. Cecilia attempts to ape Bohemian society by her flagrant smoking. Neither Robbie nor Cecilia seem to have the slightest trace of conscience about having sex outside wedlock, and Paul Marshall is equally morally indifferent about having illegal sex with the under-age Lola, who likewise accepts it, either immediately or subsequently. Jack Tallis is also having an extra-marital affair, about which he appears to feel no guilt, and which Emily tacitly accepts.

Social class

Part One of *Atonement* is set in the summer of 1935. At this time, social class remained extremely important in British society. The Second World War loosened the rigidity of class barriers, for a number of reasons: working-class children from the cities were evacuated to middle- and upper-class families in the country; all classes were equally subjected to rationing, arguably a greater suffering for the wealthy than for the poor; all shared the horrors of the Blitz; and men (and women) from all backgrounds found themselves thrown together in military units for prolonged periods of time. After the war, society in Britain changed profoundly.

The following show that the Tallis family is stereotypically upper-middle class:

- They own and live in an expensive country house with a swimming pool, a pretentious mock-Greek temple and a fountain in the landscaped grounds.
- Jack Tallis is a senior civil servant.
- The children were sent to board at public schools (both girls to Roedean; we do not know about Leon).
- The children went or are expected to go to university (Cecilia to Cambridge).

- They have domestic servants.
- They have elaborate, formal social rituals for evening drinks and dinner.

It is the ownership of their house (oddly, it does not appear to have a name) that confirms the status of the Tallis family in the eyes of others. The house and grounds also play key roles in the action of Part One. Below is a plan of the ground floor of the house and of its grounds.

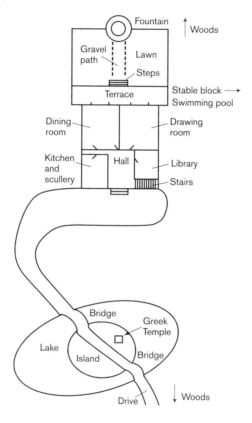

Plan of the Tallis house and grounds

Robbie Turner, by contrast, is the son of the Tallises' cleaner ('charlady'), so he is 'working class' and therefore socially inferior to them. His father, Ernest Turner, before he ran off inexplicably, was employed as the Tallises' gardener, and they lived in the 'tied cottage' (p. 87), a cottage 'tied' to the employment. His social inferiority is stressed by references to humiliating experiences at Cambridge (p. 86), reinforcing the important point that in the 1930s the sons of cleaners were not able to go to university at all, let alone to Cambridge. He was able to do so as a result of the rather patronising charitable generosity of Jack Tallis (which Emily Tallis clearly resented). The fact, clearly illustrated in Chapter 8, that he had a genuine

passion for literature is of no importance compared with his humble background; indeed, the fact that he gained a First Class degree, while Cecilia only gained a Third, is held against him, as if he is subverting the natural order by doing better than his employer's daughter. All these subtle social currents constitute the background against which the Tallis family is prepared to send him to prison for a crime for which there is no proof; keeping the 'lower orders' 'in their place' was seen as a social duty, although Jack Turner does not accept this view. Cecilia analyses these strands in a letter to Robbie: 'Now that I've broken away, I'm beginning to understand the snobbery that lay behind their stupidity. My mother never forgave you your first' (p. 209).

An aspect of this relationship, which is of particular significance for the novel, is the decision of Jack Tallis to pay for Robbie Turner's education. Jack Tallis probably views this act of generosity as an example of his superior station, evidence that he is worthy to act as 'lord of the manor' through his ownership of the house, despite his own humble origins. 'Noblesse oblige' was an important concept (nobles have obligations of social duty to be honoured), but Jack Tallis is no noble. It is a reflection upon the arrangements of the period that no poor child could go to university; higher education remained the preserve of those who could pay. Cecilia, whose 'right' to study at Cambridge depends upon the wealth of her parents (they could afford to send her to Roedean to be prepared for entry), seems to have little aptitude for higher study, nor even any particular interest in literature; how often does she give a literary reference or echo? Robbie, by contrast, is steeped in the subject, reads widely and deeply, and (at least as Briony presents him) is regularly linked with many other literary figures and works (see the section of 'Intertextuality' on pp. 84–86 of this guide). Robbie is more deserving of a Cambridge education than Cecilia, but the attitude of the remainder of the family is fundamentally hostile: Emily disapproves of Jack's 'hobby' (p. 151), Cecilia is too proud to acknowledge him while she is there, and it is impossible for Robbie to avoid feeling that Jack's charitable generosity is patronising — which it is. There are two further ways in which Jack's generosity may be viewed. One is as an example of the fashionable 'socialist' guilt of the 1930s, shared by many intellectuals including the poet Stephen Spender. Alternatively, there is an almost medieval tradition that the lord of the manor should look after the children of dead servants — translated into modern idiom, this means helping with their education.

In Part Two, Robbie has secured early release from his prison sentence in return for enlisting as a private in the infantry. His working-class status will of course have been confirmed by his imprisonment for such a crude crime as raping an under-age middle-class girl (and although he does not dwell upon it, he will no doubt have been treated very badly by the other inmates who always hate a 'nonce'). There was therefore no possibility of promotion during the short time he was in uniform. Nevertheless, in the circumstances of the defeat of the BEF and the disorderly retreat to Dunkirk, his natural qualities stand out; the two corporals, Nettle and Mace, automatically defer to him, although they are of a higher rank than he is. 'He acted like an officer, but he didn't even have a single stripe' they observe (p. 193). This is a significant comment upon the army at the time, because it was virtually impossible for a working-class man to become an officer. Robbie has natural skills, but he has also, unusually, had the middle-class opportunity of going to Cambridge, which makes him a 'fish out of water' in every class, neither properly one thing nor another, and it is a sign of the times that he suffers for this inability to conform to a class **stereotype**. Ironically, had he not been a criminal, and had he lived longer, the special circumstances of the Second World War might have led to his being commissioned as an officer, although this would have been unlikely in peacetime.

The social status of Paul Marshall is very different even from that of the Tallises. He is first referred to as 'the chocolate millionaire' (p. 26), which sets up the reader's expectations. The Tallises are wealthy, but nowhere near millionaires (a rare thing in the 1930s). This points up a subtle aspect of the British class system. The upper class was wealthy through inheriting land; the upper-middle classes were either professionals (for example, senior civil servants such as Jack Tallis) or rich business people (such as Marshall). Money acquired through trade was considered the lowest kind, and the people involved were often vulgar and uneducated. They typically attempted to 'buy class' by sending their children to private schools. Marshall, despite his money, would be viewed by many as being inferior to the Tallises, who had inherited their country house (although the family money came from a similarly commercial source) and who now held professional occupations. When Marshall appears, in Chapter 4, he is not impressive: 'I've heard an awful lot about you,' he says (p. 47). Cecilia observes him and, although he is 'so unfathomably stupid' (p. 50), she still daydreams of marrying him and carrying his children: such is the appeal of money and the lifestyle of the idle rich.

Paul Marshall is guilty of a very serious crime: the rape of an under-age girl. He nevertheless avoids punishment, while the working-class Robbie ends up in prison in his place, and some readers have seen this as a clear example of the pervasive role of class in the period. This goes to the very heart of the novel. Deeply entrenched prejudices attached particular kinds of behaviour to the different classes. Men of the upper and upper-middle classes were, by definition, 'gentlemen'; their code of honour was an essential attribute of their class status, and they would therefore, supposedly, be incapable of committing atrocities such as the rape of a 15-year-old girl. Working-class people, by contrast, were thought to be little different from animals in the crudity of their appetites and their lack of self-control. It was therefore seen as plausible for working-class characters — both Robbie and Danny — to rape a young girl, and quite unthinkable for Paul Marshall (or Leon) to do so. (In passing, of course, McEwan underlines Marshall's lack of genuine class or breeding; he is merely rich because of chocolate.) This prejudice makes it possible for the family, the

police and the courts to accept Briony's uncorroborated testimony and to imprison an innocent man. But Robbie and Cecilia are just as guilty of prejudice: they know that the rapist was not Robbie, but it never crosses their mind that it could have been anyone other than Danny, the other young working-class male in the vicinity. Their shock when Briony reveals the truth in Part Three speaks volumes. Note the **irony** that the perpetrator ends up as Lord Marshall, a prominent public figure and, allegedly, philanthropist — a testament to the sales of Amo bars (i.e. an unhealthy self-indulgence) rather than to his intelligence, erudition or moral probity.

Both Briony and Cecilia become nurses during the war, and their experiences cast interesting light upon the question of class in Britain at the time. Briony's motives are special; she is so guilty about what she has done that she feels that this is one way of making atonement. Cecilia's case is different; she took a degree in English Literature as a kind of leisure pursuit, with no intention of taking up a career, and although we are told little about the intervening years it appears that she did not work. She is more like many middle- and upper-class young women who volunteered to become nurses so that they could 'do their bit' for the war effort; others joined the military (with a very limited range of roles available). The other probationers at St Thomas's Hospital are predominantly middle class — or at least the ones Briony gravitates to are — but in peacetime nursing was a lowly occupation that few middle-class girls would have opted for. Their wartime experiences are a microcosm of the way in which shared (horrific) experiences in wartime eroded the bases of social prejudice; the nurses all had to do a similar job, regardless of their backgrounds, and saw soldiers of all classes suffering and responding in ways that did not correlate with their class origins (just as Robbie's and Cecilia's university performance did not).

Themes, motifs and symbols

Several key themes in the novel have already been discussed: 'War and peace' (pp. 57–60), 'Sex and relationships' (pp. 60–64) and 'Social class' (pp. 64–68). This section covers additional themes, motifs and symbols that run through the novel.

Atonement

Atonement, of course, is the most obvious theme in the novel. This is a fundamental concept in the Jewish and Christian religions; Yom Kippur, the Day of Atonement, is the most sacred day in the Jewish calendar, although there is no direct equivalent in the Christian calendar. The need for atonement arises when an individual has committed a crime about which they feel guilty, and for which they wish to make amends, specifically to any wronged party. Although the novel is principally about Briony's need to make atonement, she is not the only character in the novel who should atone for sins of commission or omission in connection with the unjust conviction and imprisonment of Robbie Turner.

Briony, whose false testimony was directly responsible for Robbie's conviction, has made her act of atonement her life's work. You could argue that she genuinely believed in Robbie's guilt at the time, even if that belief was based upon a mixture of childish ignorance and righteous indignation. Only subsequently (we do not learn how long it took) did she realise what she had done. She must, though, have stated with greater conviction than could be justified that the person she had seen in the darkness was Robbie. A key early part of Briony's atonement is abandoning her ambitions to go to Cambridge and choosing the humble and useful job of nursing instead ('I get the impression she's taken on nursing as a sort of penance', Cecilia says (p. 212).

The crime of Paul Marshall could be seen as considerably greater. He was, after all, an adult, and even if the sex with Lola was notionally consensual (and we will never know what actually happened, or what degree of 'persuasion' was involved) it was illegal because she was under age. To allow Robbie to go to prison when he knew the truth is unforgivable. Briony implies that he may have been troubled by this; the form that his atonement took was charitable work: 'Perhaps he's spent a lifetime making amends', Briony says in 'London, 1999' (p. 357). It is at least as likely that his charity is fashionable and self-serving, and instrumental in acquiring his title. Of Lola, Briony says dismissively: 'Nothing much was ever required of Lola after that' (p. 167). She obviously knew the truth, but it would have required superhuman courage to admit it rather than shelter behind a lie, constructed for her by Briony, which enabled her to appear as a victim rather than a co-conspirator. Briony summarises bitterly at Marshall's and Lola's wedding: 'Paul Marshall, Lola Quincey, and she, Briony Tallis, had conspired with silence and falsehoods to send an innocent man to jail' (p. 325).

The problem for all attempts at atonement for this crime is that the victims were both dead before anything practical could be done. Briony claims to have had the firm intention of doing what she could, at whatever personal cost, and was prevented from doing so only by Robbie's death, which made it futile. There is no suggestion that, whatever he may have felt, Marshall ever had any intention of putting things right for Robbie.

Robbie also feels the need for atonement. In his delirium, lying in a cellar at Bray-les-Dunes, he looks back at all the atrocities he has witnessed, and feels that he, too, is guilty of not having done enough, especially for the boy's leg in the tree (p. 192), which affected him particularly deeply at the time (see pp. 261–63).

Coming of age

There is a literary tradition of 'coming of age' novels. These novels deal with that period in adolescence when a child begins the process of becoming an adult; this is

often a memorable period, marked by life-changing experiences. Briony is 13 at the start of the novel, the archetypal age for characters in such novels. However, although the life-changing experience has taken place by the end of Part One, there is no opportunity for the reader to observe the changes that follow. By the time we next see Briony, in Part Three, she is five years older and the change is well in the past. In this, as in so many other respects, McEwan subverts the convention and the reader's expectations. Nevertheless, this is clearly a life-changing day for Briony, in that she begins to think as an adult exactly at the moment when her childishness causes disaster. In the version written retrospectively by Briony herself some years later, this is the moment at which she began to develop an adult literary sensibility, partly propelled by her witnessing the events of the day. This may, of course, be a convenient retrospective rationalisation or justification, or it may be an explanation of why Briony was so detached from reality on that day. It certainly counts as a formative experience that hastened the end of childhood (see also the section on the 'Coming of age novel' in 'Literary context' on pp. 25–26).

Bearing false witness

Briony's crime, for which she spends her life making atonement, is to have borne false witness (a biblical crime: the Ninth Commandment is 'Thou shalt not bear false witness against thy neighbour'). It has been suggested that falsehood is a key theme of the novel: almost every part of the Tallis family seems to be grounded in falsehood. Their social position, as owners of a country house, is false because the family wealth originates from a grubby, commercial success: the children's grandfather, Harry Tallis, was 'the son of a farm labourer' (p. 109) who 'grew up over an ironmonger's shop and made the family fortune with a series of patents on padlocks, bolts, latches and hasps' (p. 19). When Cecilia made 'a half-hearted start on a family tree' (p. 21), she found 'the ancestors were irretrievably sunk in a bog of farm labouring, with suspicious and confusing changes of surnames among the men, and common-law marriages unrecorded in the parish registers' (p. 21). The house, newly rebuilt by this grandfather, replaced one that was only 'Adam-style' (p. 19), so not the real thing, just as the temple was 'in the style of Nicholas Revett' (p. 72). The house is even furnished with paintings, which the family has purchased, of unknown people masquerading as illustrious ancestors: 'No one knew who these people were' (p. 126). Cecilia concludes that 'the family tree was wintry and bare, as well as rootless' (p. 109).

Furthermore, Emily is a charade as a mother, and Jack as a father and husband. It is clear that Emily is perfectly aware of the reasons why Jack stays in London during the week, but prefers not to confront or admit them. Even Cecilia is a bit of a fraud as an academic. We do not quite know how she secured her place at Cambridge, but it seems likely that being a student at Roedean, a socially elite public school, was more important than her academic ability or motivation. She only

managed to achieve a Third Class degree (being shamed by Robbie's First in the process). She enjoyed her time there, but there is no evidence that she is truly a scholar (her struggle to enjoy *Clarissa* suggests that she is not).

Misinterpretations

Much of Part One is bedevilled by characters misinterpreting the actions of others; Briony is not the only one who is guilty of this. Cecilia misinterprets the occasion when Robbie removed his shoes on entering the Tallis house. In Cecilia's account (p. 27), 'Robbie made a great show of removing his boots which weren't dirty at all… Everything he did was designed to distance her.' In Robbie's account (p. 84), he had become aware that his socks were holed, and removed them for delicacy. This was an important episode for their relationship — Cecilia believing he was deliberately provoking her by emphasising his social inferiority, he trying to avoid giving offence. It is the social differences between them, perhaps emphasised by their experiences at Cambridge, that lead to Cecilia so misinterpreting his act.

Reciprocally, Robbie misinterprets Cecilia's undressing by the pond (as does Briony, observing from afar). Cecilia does this on impulse in order to prevent Robbie from atoning for his action by retrieving the pieces of the vase; the denial is his punishment (and, arguably, sets the tone for the remainder of the novel). The breaking of the vase is itself caused by each misinterpreting the other's intentions, a consequence of the unresolved tension between them. Lying in his bath that evening, Robbie concludes 'The idea was to humiliate him' (p. 80).

Briony, of course, misinterprets the fountain scene, the letter, the library scene and the rape. The critic Brian Finney says: 'Every time a character misinterprets the situation it proves to be the consequence of a projection on his or her part onto another character' (see Finney's critique listed in 'Further study' on p. 104 of this guide). At the root of all these misinterpretations is a set of misunderstandings of a fundamental nature: Cecilia cannot grasp what Robbie feels for her — or she for him — because of prejudices based upon the class difference between them. Briony's misinterpretations derive from her youth and arrogance, her heightened view of herself as novelist and observer, a misplaced desire to protect her elder sister and possibly a complex jealousy deriving from her earlier feelings for Robbie. All of these conspire to support her systematic misreading of the events of the day, with tragic consequences.

The country-house novel

Some critics have described *Atonement* as a 'country-house novel'. The setting reinforces comparisons with L. P. Hartley's novel *The Go-Between*, also set in a country house in a stiflingly hot June, and centring around an illicit passion between the daughter of the owner and a local working-class man. A child is critically involved (the character is named Leo, echoing Leon) as a go-between in this disastrous affair.

However, there are fundamental differences, and it could be argued that *Atonement* is, in fact, a parody or a travesty of a country-house novel, because the (un-named) Tallis house is in every sense a fake. *The Go-Between* is set in a genuine country house, still owned by an aristocratic family with 500 acres of adjacent land, through which the young Leo has to run to reach the farm of tenant farmer Ted Burgess, a situation barely changed since the middle ages (although the house has been rented by a London banking family, the Maudsleys, who are seeking the social cachet to go with their wealth by marrying their daughter to the owner of the house). The Tallises, by contrast, a family of no social distinction, own a tasteless modern house with left-over features from a second-rate earlier house; they have limited grounds, and Robbie is the son of a cleaner.

Parallel or symmetrical motifs

The critic Brian Finney describes how 'McEwan also draws attention to the constructed nature of the narrative by employing parallel or symmetrical motifs' (see 'Further study' on p. 104 of this guide). Marshall's rape of Lola takes place by the Greek-style, eighteenth-century, 'crumbling, stuccoed temple' (p. 19) in the Tallis grounds with its 'row of pillars and the pediment above them' (p. 72). The wedding of Marshall and Lola takes place at a London church that looks 'like a Greek temple', especially its 'low portico with white columns beneath a clocktower of harmonious proportions' (p. 323). A link is therefore established between the rape and the marriage by this similarity. Again, the next occasion on which we witness Briony encountering the Marshalls, in 'London, 1999', 'takes place outside the Imperial War Museum, which echoes the other two buildings in being based on Greek temple design and featuring columns and a portico. Behind the neo-classical facades that come to represent the "mausoleum of their marriage" [p. 325] lurk respectively ruin, a joint lie, and the destructive memories of a war from which Marshall made his fortune' (Finney). Note also the **irony** of Greek architectural motifs being used in a monument to war: we usually think of Greek architecture as representing harmony and civilisation.

The Meissen vase

The Meissen vase also serves as a symbol in the novel. Brian Finney comments on:

> ...the way McEwan uses the Meissen vase to imply connections between the specific incident of its breakage and a number of wider fractures in the narrative and the world it depicts. At the most intimate level the vase suggests the fragility of Cecilia's virgin state which is about to be as abruptly destroyed by a struggle between herself and Robbie as is the vase. The vase next enters Briony's first attempt at fiction, *Two Figures by a Fountain*, and becomes associated with her incorrect interpretation of the events leading to its rupture. Briony's testimony both in court and in her first narrative draft is as fragile as the mended vase, as McEwan subtly suggests when describing her initial determination of the identity of Lola's attacker: 'the glazed surface of her conviction was not without

its blemishes and hairline cracks' (168). Both the vase and the novel as a whole represent a fragile aesthetic form that can easily fall apart. During the War it is finally shattered, just as the Tallis family's way of life is shattered by historical events which cause its extinction. This takes one back to the first description of the vase: it was a gift awarded to Jack Tallis's brother Clem during the First World War which, despite wartime conditions, survived and was brought back to the Tallis family after his death in action. Valuable as it is, Jack Tallis wants it to be used: 'If it had survived the war, the reasoning went, then it could survive the Tallises' (24). In other words the vase is a fragile object which has miraculously survived two centuries of use (as has the structured society that the Tallises represent), and which is directly identified with the family through Uncle Clem. Its fracturing and eventual destruction anticipate those of the family and the pre-War society to which both belong. (See Finney's critique listed in 'Further study' on p. 104 of this guide.)

It can be argued that the vase means more than this: it is a symbol of preciousness, and it is ironic that it is a product of German civilisation. It was acquired by Uncle Clem to save it from being destroyed by the Germans themselves during the First World War, and it is destroyed during the next conflict, which is again against the Germans. The flowers which Cecilia places in it, doomed to die after a brief glory, can be seen as a symbol for virginity and young women, who bloom only for a short time in their desirable prime.

Language, style and structure

Now that it is apparent that, despite appearances to the contrary, Parts One, Two and Three of *Atonement* constitute the (final?) text of Briony's life's work — her fictional account of the events of 1935 and their consequences for the principal protagonists — it is important to examine their language, style and structure. (Whatever the status of 'London, 1999', it does not appear to be part of the novel, as it discusses it in a way which would be self-referential to the point of imploding if it were.)

The style of Part One is quite consistent, notwithstanding the range of viewpoints, and this leads the reader to presume that it is the voice of McEwan that they are hearing, taking on the viewpoint of the various characters. When it transpires that this is the work of Briony, the same argument applies; the consistency reflects the single hand at work. Although this may cast doubt upon some of what is reported, stylistically there is consistency. McEwan himself has described the style of this part as 'a slightly mannered prose, slightly held in, a little formal, a tiny bit archaic' (quoted in Finney; see 'Further study' on p. 104 of this guide).

The events of Part Two are very different in nature from those of Part One, and the style of the writing reflects this. McEwan has claimed that in Part Two, writing about Dunkirk, he chose 'to write in a choppier prose with shorter, simpler sentences', a style that is reminiscent of Hemingway. As he explained, 'on

the battlefield the subordinate clause has no place' (quoted in Finney). This can be detected by noting the more sparing use of adjectives, and the more frequent use of short, factual sentences, e.g. 'He sat up and looked at his watch' (p. 214) — a narrative sentence that would have no place in Part One.

The language of Part Three is similar to that of Part One; it is literary and sophisticated, as you would expect from the mature Briony reflecting upon events that happened years before. This has the effect of making the narrative less immediate and more reflective, but it should be noted that when the casualties arrive at the hospital, the style resembles Part Two, with shorter narrative sentences.

'London, 1999' is not part of what turns out to be Briony's carefully crafted novel but a memoir, and as a consequence the style of this section is different. Apart from anything else, it is written in the first person. Although it is mostly in the past tense, the very final section, set in her room in the Tilney Hotel after the entertainment has finally made *The Trials of Arabella* a reality, is written in the present tense and gives a powerful sense of bringing the reader right up to date with the story as it is unfolding. This gives immediacy to round off a novel that has, until now, been told at a considerable historical distance.

The structure of the novel (or perhaps novels) is distinctive, in that it consists of a series of episodes seemingly abstracted from a larger history. The longest section, Part One, concerns itself with the events of little more than one day, but by virtue of the number of viewpoints included, a substantial amount of essential background material is conveyed. Part One ends with Robbie being driven away in a police car, and with Grace Turner ominously and accurately shouting 'Liars! Liars!' (p. 187) (for it turned out that there were, in the end, more than one liar).

There is no link helping the reader to understand the transition to Part Two, five years later, in another country and another voice, and only slowly does enough background filter out for the reader to identify the voice and the setting, inferring that Robbie was indeed imprisoned for the 'rape' — an outcome by no means certain at the end of the previous section. Part Two also leaves the reader in suspense, this time with two possible outcomes hanging evenly in the balance: Nettle has announced that they are to be marched to a boat at seven, but at the same time the reader is acutely aware of Robbie's deteriorating physical state.

Part Three, again, seems for a long time unconnected to what has preceded it, although the identity of the narrating voice and the situation are more immediately apparent. Only after a considerable time does the connection with Part Two become apparent, but the climax of this section may also be viewed as the climax of the novel. In this the role of the title must be taken into account, so the reader is expecting some 'atonement' from Briony for 'her crime' (her own words, of course, transferred to the third person, p. 156). The reunion of the key actors, Briony, Cecilia and Robbie, is emotionally charged, and it might be thought that Briony gets off lightly for what

she has done, even if Cecilia avers 'I won't ever forgive you' (p. 337). There are dark hints at the end of this section; Robbie is returning to his unit for combat duty, and the future tragedy that is to claim Cecilia's life is bluntly referred to (although without the connection being stated). Nevertheless, the reader comes to the end of this section with, they think, a reasonable understanding of 'what happened': Marshall's role is clear, and Briony has begun the process of atoning for her error. But within seconds, all that is cruelly undermined by the signature 'BT London 1999', instantly calling into question the veracity of the whole thing.

The reader's suspicions are confirmed in the succeeding section, 'London, 1999', in which Briony begins to talk explicitly about the process of researching and writing her novel — which is what the previous sections prove to have been. It is only a few pages before the bombshell is dropped, on p. 370, that 'Robbie Turner died of septicaemia at Bray Dunes on 1 June 1940', thus subverting the status of the whole of Part Three, and especially its climactic scene. But although this epilogue clearly has a different status from the three preceding parts, as it is not part of the novel to which it refers, it still plays with the reader: Briony does not say, in so many words, which version was the truth; only that 'All the preceding drafts were pitiless' (p. 370), and that she can 'no longer think what purpose would be served' (p. 370) if she were to have Robbie and Cecilia die. This does not state what happened; it invites the reader to infer, and at the same time raises the fundamental question of what she, the novelist is doing, what ends she serves. In a sense, 'what purpose?' is the novel's fundamental question.

A number of critics have complained about significant omissions in *Atonement*: many key events and episodes are not presented to the reader at all, or only indirectly through retrospective references. This is presumably part of McEwan's **Postmodernist** agenda to deny readers the satisfaction they seek. It would be too conventional to tell the 'whole story', so McEwan/Briony choose the episodes that they decide to tell, and leave the reader to fill in the gaps from the shreds of evidence that exist.

Most readers would like to know more about the trial, perhaps being given the scenes in which Briony testifies or Cecilia (presumably) defends Robbie's behaviour. They would also like to witness the point(s) at which Briony's certainty crumbles, and learn the incidents or ideas that lead her from her childish conviction to the point, in Part Three, where she describes her behaviour as 'the terrible thing that I did' (p. 340). It would also have been interesting to have an account of any of the encounters between Marshall and Lola after the very first; what did happen between the 'rape' and the marriage? How long was allowed to lapse before Marshall dared contact her again, and subsequently allow his feelings to become public knowledge?

As Part Two is told from Robbie's viewpoint, it would not be possible to include his death, and if he were dead there would be little point in Part Three as its dramatic climax would be impossible. And although the reader might like to know more about Briony's life and career after 1940, especially the episode of her

marriage (where is Thierry now? How did it happen? Why no children?), it is all tangential to the central concern of the novel — Briony's crime.

The letter from Cyril Connolly to Briony in Part Three is structurally important. This is the point at which a perceptive reader may begin to suspect the true status of the whole novel. From the comments made by Connolly, it is possible to form a fair view of the immature and romantic story submitted by the young Briony; it also allows the reader to see how far the final draft — i.e. Part One — has not only developed, but also how far Connolly's comments have shaped it. This gives a glimpse of the creative process of the novelist; and it may also make the reader question how far Briony needed such guidance in order to craft a text of the quality of the one we are given. The crucial, and perhaps worrying, part comes where Connolly makes suggestions for improvement of the draft: 'If this girl has so fully misunderstood or been so wholly baffled by the strange little scene that has unfolded before her, how might it affect the lives of the two adults? Might she come between them in some disastrous fashion?' (p. 313). There then follow other suggestions that are not taken up in the novel we have (including, as a direct homage to *The Go-Between*, 'Might the young couple come to use her as a messenger?', p. 313). But if the possibility that Briony might 'come between them' is a suggestion of Connolly's, in what sense can the reader be confident that any of the story is based on 'actual' events in Briony's life? But if it is not, why has she dedicated her life to this act of atonement? Why can she not publish during the lifetime of Lord and Lady Marshall? Although this adds to the Postmodernist uncertainty in the reader's mind, on balance it seems as if, in this one suggestion out of several, Connolly merely chances to hit upon what actually transpired.

The novel employs a device known as **prolepsis** or narrative anticipation, where the narrative knowingly looks forward from the point of narration to future events. The most striking example comes at the opening of Chapter 13: 'Within the half hour Briony would commit her crime' (p. 156). A more subtle, but perhaps more revealing, example comes earlier, when Briony discusses her response to witnessing the scene by the fountain (which was to be the subject, and even the title, of the very first draft of her novel, *Two Figures by a Fountain*):

> The definition would refine itself over the years. She was to concede that she may have attributed more deliberation than was feasible to her thirteen-year-old self. At the time there may have been no precise form of words; in fact she may have experienced nothing more than impatience to begin writing again. (p. 40)

She then goes on to interpolate:

> Six decades later she would describe how at the age of thirteen she had written her way through a whole history of literature…to arrive at an impartial psycho-logical realism which she had discovered for herself, one special morning during a heat wave in 1935. (p. 41)

This is prolepsis on a grand scale. Its effect, of course, is to interrupt the momentum of the narration of events as they occurred, to break the tension and remind the reader that they are being written, many years later, with the benefit of hindsight. It is occasionally applied to other characters as well, e.g. Emily, about Jack: 'She did not mind, for he would be back at the weekend, and one day he would be home for ever and not an unkind word would be spoken' (p. 153). Here, also, it imparts a retrospective feel to the narrative.

Viewpoint and voice

Atonement is a novel, above all, about writing fiction: the process, the consequences and the limitations. It appears to include multiple viewpoints and voices, and in a sense by the end it both does and does not. It is a challenge for a student to come to grips with these complexities.

At a first reading (and it should of course be borne in mind that the great majority of readers read a novel only once), the impression is created that McEwan is narrating a story in a conventional, third-person, past-tense narrative, albeit from the viewpoints of several of the key participants. Arguably, it is only when the reader arrives at the epilogue/coda, 'London, 1999', that doubt is cast on the status of the narrative up to this point. It is useful to think back to your first reading of the text and to consider how you responded to it at that time.

It has been stated that Part One of *Atonement* is a classic 'realist narration' with multiple narrative viewpoints. It appears to give a 'neutral' account of events, related in the past tense by the author. He adopts the viewpoint of one of the characters for each chapter, but stylistically they are consistent, as are the events that are narrated. The reader supposes that the author employed multiple viewpoints to increase the reader's involvement with the unfolding events. It can be described as 'realist' because it simply recounts the events of the day, illuminated by the thoughts of the key participants and with some insights into the background. The events are told more or less in order, with some slight overlaps when the same events are related by more than one character. The events take place over a period of little more than a day, and there are no significant time-leaps.

However, as early as Chapter 3 the reference to what Briony would do and think 'six decades later' (p. 41) may lead the perceptive reader to question the status of the narrative, because this observation is out of place in a 'realist narration'. Again, in Chapter 11 (p. 139) Robbie reconstructs with implausible accuracy the sequence of thoughts that went through Briony's mind in the library. In Chapter 14, when Briony refers to 'her own vile excitement' (p. 173), this is clearly a judgement that 'belongs' much later in the story and has 'slipped' into this early section.

Similarly, it has been suggested that Parts Two and Three can also be read as a realist narration (i.e. a novel narrated by Ian McEwan). Part Two, because it is narrated entirely in the **persona** of Robbie, gives no obvious grounds for suspicion; there are no incongruities, and the narration seems coloured by Robbie's experiences of the war, as well as containing convincing military and contextual references that support this view of authorship. It is a chronological account, with some flashbacks to fill in the gaps. Part Three is also the work of a single voice, in this case Briony's, and is chronological and consistent. The only point that might give rise to concern comes in the final section, when she says 'she felt the distance widen between her and another self, no less real, who was walking back towards the hospital' (p. 329). There is a slight air of unreality about this whole scene, accentuated by the strange suggestion: 'Perhaps the Briony who was walking in the direction of Balham was the imagined or ghostly persona' (p. 329). This comes as close as Briony can to giving a hint of what she is to admit just a few pages later (p. 370), that the visit to Balham is made up.

The effect of the words 'BT London 1999', which appear at the end of Part Three on p. 349, give the game away (or confirm the reader's increasing suspicions). Unless the unwary reader thinks this is an incomprehensible reference to British Telecom, it must instantly be clear that the initials are those of 'Briony Tallis', acknowledging authorship and composition date of the section which, up to that moment, had masqueraded as the fiction of Ian McEwan, in which she was a mere character. It causes the reader to reconsider the status of the whole of Part Three, although that is in any case Briony's narrative. But it also calls into question (justifiably, as it turns out shortly afterwards) the authorship and status of Part Two, and even Part One.

As the reader reads 'London, 1999' it becomes increasingly apparent that their assumptions about the nature of Parts One to Three are being undermined, and finally completely confounded. The whole tone and style of 'London, 1999' are clearly different from Parts One to Three, but in any case the words 'BT London 1999', immediately prior to this section, have alerted the reader to the true situation. It is clearly a memoir, by the author Briony, and not part of the novel that has preceded it. She describes her craft and actions as a novelist, including researching the Second World War section at the Imperial War Museum. On p. 356 she explains that she conflated the three hospitals at which she nursed for Part Three, introducing the idea that she is going to confide a series of revealing, authorial secrets about the novel that, it is increasingly obvious, constituted Parts One to Three. The references to the Marshalls (p. 356) and Mr Nettle (p. 359) confirm the relationship between Briony and the novel. Finally, on pp. 370–71, Briony admits the truth about what 'really' happened and the degree of fictionalisation of her account. The truth about the death of Robbie is, of course, the greatest surprise; the subsequent death of Cecilia, although no doubt tragic, does not alter the novel we are given because it took place after Briony's imaginary meeting with her and Robbie in Balham.

Having read 'London, 1999', the reader must reassess the whole of the remainder of the novel in the light of what it contains. Most fundamentally, Part One needs to be re-assessed. Part Three can still be seen as broadly autobiographical, except for the meeting with Cecilia and Robbie, which has in any case been signposted as questionable (as indicated above). Part Two needs no revision; a revisiting of the ambiguous ending can be seen as perfectly consistent with Robbie's illness having overtaken him during the final night, robbing him of the escape from the beaches promised for the following morning. Part One, however, has to be seen in a completely new light. If the whole narrative is Briony's, then those sections purporting to reflect the thoughts and perspectives of other characters — eight chapters out of 14 — suddenly lose their presumed veracity and become at best an educated guess and at worst deliberate attempts by Briony to construct a narrative that suits her purposes. They are plainly manipulative, and the question of Briony's motivation, and the impression she is seeking to establish by using other voices in this way, becomes paramount. It is at this point that the gaps in the novel become important: the reader does not know whether Briony ever spoke to Cecilia before her death, or when she became reconciled with her family. It is reasonable to assume that she was able to investigate the events of 1935 exhaustively in the years that followed, and that she carefully selected the story she unfolds. Her reconstruction of the states of mind of Cecilia and Robbie during that fateful day must be entirely speculative, and this is arguably where the reader's initial reactions are most likely to be questioned.

In the light of 'London, 1999', it now seems that what 'really' happened in the story of Briony, Cecilia and Robbie is as follows. Paul Marshall, having earlier attempted to molest Lola in the playroom (where she clearly resisted, hence the scratches), met up with her during the search (we do not know whether this was agreed in advance; on balance it probably was) where he proceeded to rape or possibly seduce her. Whether Lola struggled or consented is not clear, but at some point — arguably during the conversation with Briony — she decided to protect Marshall's identity by going along with Briony's determination to incriminate Robbie. Briony, although possibly feeling increasingly uncomfortable, stuck to her story and the jury convicted Robbie. They were almost certainly more influenced by the evidence of the sexually explicit letter (which, of course, they only knew about because Briony sought it out and gave it to the police — her other, less remembered 'crime' of the evening) than that of a small girl in the darkness, but probably also by the class assumptions. Robbie was let off part of his sentence (he served 4 years) by volunteering for the infantry. There was one rather tense meeting with Cecilia before he departed for France, never to return, although he came cruelly close to evacuation from Dunkirk. Briony attended the wedding of Marshall and Lola, which was probably the point at which she appreciated what had really happened. By then, although she had written to Cecilia to volunteer to change her testimony, it was too late because Robbie was

already dead. Cecilia was killed a few months later in the raid on Balham, so Briony was probably unable to be reconciled with her, and the novel, her life's work, was undertaken as a form of atonement to their memories. As the decades passed the novel came to take on a life of its own, and by the end its significance for her became almost metaphysical.

Briony suggests in 'London, 1999' that there were other (earlier) drafts of the novel in which a meeting took place after Robbie's death, and it is instructive to imagine how Briony might have presented such a meeting. The difficulty with this idea is that if Robbie had died, and they were both aware of it, then there would be no point in having the scene at all; there would be no useful atonement that Briony could make, and no reason for Cecilia to control her rage. In fact, there is no possibility that Briony would have gone to see Cecilia under such circumstances, so the fictional version may be the only one that allows Briony and Cecilia to encounter one another again. It is dramatically important because it allows Briony to tell the other two what really happened on the fateful night. (Another possibility might be that Briony arrives at Cecilia's flat just at the moment when she receives news of Robbie's death at Dunkirk; such a scene would, however, give no opportunity for reconciliation or clarification.)

In the context of the novel's construction of events, it is also relevant to consider what Briony's sources would have been for the narrative she constructs. Briony herself witnessed the court process and conviction of Robbie at first hand. (Why does this not feature in the novel? The dramatic potential is considerable.) It is clear that she resumed contact with her brother Leon at some point, although he is not mentioned in Part Three, and he would have given her ample information about subsequent events. Although she had no contact with Robbie, she may have had access to his letters to Cecilia (although she does not say so). She certainly had contact with 'Mr Nettle' (p. 359), which would have given her a basis for Part Two. Part Three recounts her own experiences, except for the part that is imaginary.

All this leads to the reader having considerable reservations about the concept of 'what really happened' in the context of this novel. In traditional fiction the role of the author is to tell a story, which is consistent and convincing, and for which the reader chooses to suspend disbelief (i.e. the reader pretends that the story is true and not fiction). The **Postmodernists** subverted this cosy relationship, and typically failed to deliver the story that the reader was hoping for. *Atonement* is firmly in this tradition. By giving the impression initially that it tells a traditional story, and then subsequently revealing that it is not what it seems, it confounds the reader's expectation of reading a simple story. Nevertheless, there is a (more complex) story that can be described as constituting the novel *Atonement*: it is Briony's fictionalised account of Briony's crime and its consequences. This is a fiction of Ian McEwan: Briony Tallis is a fictional creation, who happens to be a novelist. The way McEwan chooses to present this fictional character is in the form of one of her novels, which she reveals in the postscript to be

semi-autobiographical (as most novels are). In this same postscript, 'London, 1999', McEwan has Briony reflect on the nature of fiction and the power of the novelist, and it is this that causes the reader to reflect. The reader is brought to believe that Briony and Cecilia and Robbie are real characters whose fate they wish to find out about. The character Briony chooses to involve the reader in her claim that these events 'really' happened in her (fictional) world, and that 'her' novel is an attempt to atone for them. It is these layers of fictionality that can cause the reader to question what is actually being offered. The term **metafiction** is often employed to refer to works of fiction such as *Atonement*, which explicitly discuss the devices and methods of writing fiction.

When the reader knows that Part One of the novel is the retrospective, fiction-alised account of Briony rather than a realist narrative by McEwan, the belief initially engendered that this is a relatively objective account written by an 'omniscient narrator' (i.e. McEwan) turns out to be unsustainable. The determined reader will go back and read this section again in the knowledge that, notwithstanding the appearance of a range of viewpoints, all are actually those of Briony; the thoughts and emotions attributed to the other characters immediately become unreliable. They are, at best, Briony's honestly intended reconstruction, with hindsight, from outside (bearing in mind that she did not witness most of these scenes); at worst, they are entirely contrived by her to lend colour and supporting detail to the fictions she has constructed to flesh out her account of the events leading up to Robbie's arrest. As we do not know how far she would have been able to discuss this with the other characters, we do not know how much of it is inevitably fiction. And given her own, rather damning statement in 'London, 1999' that 'If I really cared so much about facts, I should have written a different kind of book' (p. 360), the reader must suspect that she will have fabricated as necessary to suit her purposes.

Similar arguments apply to Parts Two and Three. As we know that Briony could not have spoken to Robbie again, the detailed account in Part Two, especially, including as it does extensive comments on Robbie's state of mind, must be wholly fictitious in quite a different way from that assumed by the reader on a first reading. It is implied, in 'London, 1999', that it is based to a significant degree on 'my dozen long letters from old Mr Nettle' (p. 353) — a very different kind of material from which to construct such a narrative. Part Three, as Briony's autobiographical account of her war years, at least has the possibility of reflecting 'reality', as she was in a position to know what Briony thought and experienced. She signposts clearly enough where her account diverges from 'reality' when, on p. 329, she writes 'she felt the distance widen between her and another self, no less real, who was walking back towards the hospital'.

Ultimately, the effect of these revelations about the authorship of the novel is to serve McEwan's **Postmodernist** intention of preventing readers from thinking they have read a conventional novel that tells 'a story'; he explicitly draws attention to the status of fiction, and the role of the novelist, by these devices.

A further complication results from consideration of gender. By implying that the whole novel is written by Briony, when in fact it was written by McEwan, a gender ambiguity is introduced. This is significant in the sense that, although it has historically been relatively common for male writers to adopt a female **persona**, it is unusual for the reverse to happen. However, the novel purports to be exactly that: the work of Briony, a female author, writing in the persona of various male characters, especially Robbie Turner, in Parts One and Two. The reader must judge how successfully this enterprise has been executed. The reader may also speculate upon why women writers so rarely attempt to adopt a male voice — do they consider it too presumptuous? How many male authors really display sufficient insight into the female psyche for their representations to carry conviction?

Postmodernism and intertextuality

McEwan has always had a strong interest in the business of writing novels and the power of the novelist. *Atonement* is the work in which he most explicitly addresses these issues. What appears at first to be a conventional story told by an omniscient narrator (i.e. McEwan), albeit from the viewpoints of the characters involved, turns out to be nothing of the kind. It is 'in fact' Briony's novel, her life's work, in which she attempts to make atonement for the crime she 'actually' committed at the age of 13; its ramifications are worked out through the remainder of the novel. But because the novel is about the writing of the novel, which it itself is, it is self-referential to a rare degree ('a fiction within a fiction'). It is one of the characteristic features of Postmodernism to subvert the reader's expectations, and to deny them the satisfaction of being told a story in which they can believe. Briony/McEwan has included in the published novel the version of Part Three that, we are explicitly told, is not 'true' (i.e. does not reflect what 'actually' happened in the core story upon which the novels are based); this fact highlights the ways in which novelists, acting like God, can manipulate both their characters and, through them, their readers. The postscript, 'London, 1999', makes a number of these points explicitly, to ensure that even an insensitive reader cannot fail to see that there is a paradox.

Briony's novel and Postmodernism

Is Ian McEwan's novel *Atonement* in fact Briony Tallis's last novel, still to be published? We are not told the title of this work. We do know that the early version rejected by *Horizon* magazine was entitled *Two Figures by a Fountain*, but this dealt with the first episode of the story only. The presumption must be that it is, to some

degree, the novel that is published as *Atonement*, but there are problems with this — not least the 1999 postscript in which Briony gives away too much about the choices she has made between alternative versions and, critically, undermines Part Three as we have it.

What is clear is that this novel has preoccupied her throughout her life, and it is an act of atonement for her great childhood crime. In order to succeed in this purpose, it needs to bear some resemblance to the truth, and it is apparent that this is a real issue for Briony ('the least of my offences against veracity', p. 356). She discusses the novel extensively in the 1999 postscript, and in this section she appears to be telling 'the truth' about what 'actually' happened in the underlying story of the novel(s). If, however, the novel *Atonement* is Briony's last novel, then it is clearly not true, as she claims, that 'There would be no further drafts' (p. 360), because she incorporated all the corrections offered by the 'obliging old colonel of the Buffs' (p. 359). Perhaps they do not constitute a new draft.

What the postscript is about, and therefore what the novel is about, is the whole business of fiction, and the role and power of the novelist. McEwan plays with the reader, just as Briony plays with the reader on his behalf. A traditional novel tells a story, but the Postmodernist novel typically denies the reader the satisfaction of finding out 'what happened'. The whole conception of *Atonement* causes the reader to consider explicitly the relationship between the novelist and the novel. In Parts One, Two and Three, right up to the final word, the reader may presume that they are being offered a novel by Ian McEwan that tells, from multiple viewpoints, a single coherent and consistent story, that this is what happened in the consistent fictional universe that he has created. Up to the end of p. 349 (94% of the length of the novel) this impression is sustainable and reasonable. It is then suddenly subverted (with what magisterial economy!) by the sign-off at the end: 'BT London 1999'. Assuming readers are sufficiently alert to understand this code, they are jolted out of their preconceptions and required to re-evaluate everything that has passed. If all this has been Briony's account — and, as is about to be reinforced, but we already know, she is a novelist — then this is not McEwan's consistent story but Briony's version of the events in which she played a part so central and destructive that there is no possibility of the account being in any simple sense 'true'.

For Briony, writing the novel clearly constitutes an attempt at atonement for her crime. Conventional atonement typically requires an act of restitution to the wronged party or parties. We know that Briony intended to do this, as far as lay in her power, i.e. to go through the humiliation of formally recanting her evidence (thereby running the risk of, at worst, a perjury charge) in the hope of restoring Robbie's reputation even if she could not restore the lost years. Fate cheated her of the opportunity of doing this when Robbie died at Bray-les-Dunes, and the possibility of giving Cecilia some satisfaction by posthumously redeeming Robbie's reputation was also lost when Cecilia in turn was killed by the Balham bomb some months later. With both victims

of her 'crime' dead, Briony concluded that there remained only one way in which any form of atonement could be made; the argument is well made by McEwan himself in an interview:

> When this novel is published [after her death] these two lovers will survive to love, and they will survive spontaneous, fortuitous Cecilia and her medical prince right out of the little playlet she was trying to write at the age of thirteen. They will always live. (Quoted in Finney: see 'Further study' on p. 104 of this guide.)

This is a powerful statement of the view that literature and myth can immortalise lives that would otherwise be lost for ever.

The novel begins and ends with Briony's play, *The Trials of Arabella*, a thinly disguised moral tale, written for Leon but actually about Cecilia. Just as the heroine allows herself to fall victim to a 'reckless passion' (p. 3), so might Cecilia, but Arabella is allowed a second chance with a 'medical prince' (p. 3) — suggesting that the medical dimension is already of interest to Briony, possibly because Robbie has announced his ambitions in that field. The play acts as a framing motif for the novel: at the outset it is in prospect, a symbol of Bryony's precocious and immature ambition; when it is finally performed, 64 years later, it brings to a formal close an episode and a life. The choice of name for the heroine is also significant (see below).

Intertextuality

A characteristic feature of **Postmodernist** fiction is the idea of **intertextuality** — that a fictional work should pay homage to earlier works of literature, by direct quotation or indirect reference or echo. Many critics have noted that *Atonement* is a richly intertextual text.

Among the texts referred to in the novel, Jane Austen's *Northanger Abbey* has pride of place because of its prominent position in the **epigraph**. In this novel Catherine Morland is told off by Henry Tilney for making trouble as a result of her over-active imagination. As McEwan himself put it in an interview, it is a novel 'about someone's wild imagination causing havoc to people around them' (quoted in Finney). As Brian Finney puts it, 'Tilney's remarks to Catherine ("what ideas have you been admitting?") can be applied equally fittingly to Briony, whose equally over-active imagination leads her to tell the crucial lie.' The renaming of the Tallis house as 'Tilney's Hotel' reinforces the connection (although, of course, only a well-read reader would recognise it). Henry Tilney is a key character in *Northanger Abbey* (he represents reason and reality), so it is fitting that his name should be associated with this novel. It is also telling that, following the death of Emily, the house was sold. Presumably no member of the family wished to live in it, and no private purchaser could be found — the implication being perhaps that it was so ugly and lacking in architectural interest that a hotel was the only suitable use for it. Even for that major changes were needed, including removing the ornamental lake.

The name strengthens the intertextual link with *Northanger Abbey* at the very end of the novel, having established it at the outset.

There are many other examples of intertextuality in the novel. The repeated references to the exceptional heat, the country house setting and the role of the child in the sexual liaisons of the adults all directly invoke L. P. Hartley's *The Go-Between*, in which the hot summer days lead to a similar mixture of listlessness, heightened sexual appetite and reduced inhibitions. (In both cases, this leads to the key female character removing her clothes in order to enter water.)

The name Arabella for the heroine of Briony's play also suggests a literary echo: she is a central character in Richardson's novel *Clarissa*, which Cecilia is attempting to read — and making hard work of — and which Robbie loved (further pointing up the gap in literary sensitivity between them). Richardson's novel is also concerned with a rape — that of Clarissa herself — and is a further literary parallel to the rape of Lola. Here the rape leads to the death of Clarissa and the subsequent death of the rapist, as was customary; yet another convention is overturned by McEwan in making the rape the route to the successful marriage and social success of Paul and Lola.

Robbie, immersed in literary texts, quotes Malvolio from *Twelfth Night*: 'nothing that can be can come between me and the full prospect of my hopes' (p. 131) (which are to climb socially by getting into Olivia's bed). This hubristic quotation may suggest to the reader that Robbie may prove as deluded as Malvolio was. Similarly, on his journey to Dunkirk, Robbie quotes a line from one of Cecilia's letters: '*In the nightmare of the dark, All the dogs of Europe bark*' (p. 203). McEwan does not point it out, but this is a line from W. H. Auden's poem 'In Memory of W. B. Yeats' – a doubly intertextual reference.

Attempting to explain to Cecilia, in the library, how he had sent her the 'wrong' version of his letter, Robbie is minded (rather pretentiously, you might think) to refer to 'the Orioli edition of *Lady Chatterley's Lover*' (p. 132) — not only as an explanation for the explicit sexuality, but also as an echo of a lower-class man who seduces an upper-class woman. Another explicit reference is to a very different kind of text: *Gray's Anatomy*, ostensibly part of his preparation for a medical career, but tellingly open at 'page 1546, the vagina' (p. 94). These, and all the other references to Robbie's reading in this chapter, place him firmly in the literary traditions that have shaped his sensibility.

The appearance of Cyril Connolly in the letter about Briony's first draft is an extended intertextual reference (he is identified only as 'CC'; the less discerning reader may well not guess that this is a reference to a real magazine and its famous editor, unless they remember the passing reference by Cecilia on p. 212). The letter suggests that Briony has been too much influenced by 'the techniques of Mrs Woolf' (i.e. Virginia Woolf; p. 312), and then says that Elizabeth Bowen read the manuscript. Although now little known, Bowen was a highly regarded novelist at the time, and her novel *The Heat of the Day* has been acknowledged by McEwan as

one of his inspirations when writing *Atonement*. Another of her works, *The Demon Lover*, set in the London Blitz in the Second World War, tells the story of a dead soldier who returns to reclaim his lover. The inclusion of real historical characters in a fiction is characteristic of another Postmodernist device, sometimes called **faction**.

McEwan has also acknowledged a debt to Henry James's *What Maisie Knew*, and has stated :

> I didn't want to write about a child's mind with the limitations of a child's vocabulary or a child's point of view. I wanted to be more like [Henry] James in *What Maisie Knew*: to use the full resources of an adult mentality remembering herself. (Quoted in Finney: see 'Further study' on p. 104 of this guide.)

Among many other intertextual references that have been suggested, the naming of the nymphet willing rape victim as Lola is surely an echo of Vladimir Nabokov's *Lolita*. Note also the list of pairs of literary lovers that Robbie gives on p. 204.

The power of the novelist

In 'London, 1999' Briony writes at length about the power and dilemmas of the novelist (pp. 369–71). She describes what she has done: 'I've been thinking about my last novel, the one that should have been my first….There was our crime — Lola's, Marshall's, mine — and from the second version onwards, I set out to describe it' (p. 369). She calls it a 'forensic memoir' (p. 370), but immediately subverts this by saying 'It is only in this last version that my lovers end well' (p. 370). She then lists all the reasons why she could not bear to stick with the truthful version of the story: 'How could that constitute an ending? What sense or hope or satisfaction could a reader draw from such an account?' (p. 371). This comment draws reader attention to the question of the moral aim of literature, a question of particular importance to McEwan. Embedded in this is Briony's, and presumably McEwan's, credo as a novelist. 'When I am dead, and the Marshalls are dead, and the novel is finally published, we will only exist as my inventions' (p. 371). This is the power of the novelist. 'No one will care what events and which individuals were misrepresented to make a novel' (p. 371). This is where a novel differs from a memoir or a history: emotional truth is what matters, not literal truth.

> I know there's always a certain kind of reader who will be compelled to ask, But what *really* happened? The answer is simple: the lovers survive and flourish. As long as there is a single copy, a solitary typescript of my final draft, then my spontaneous, fortuitous sister and her medical prince survive to love. (p. 371)

But then she moves on to the dilemma and the problem: 'The problem these fifty-nine years has been this: how can a novelist achieve atonement when, with her absolute power of determining outcomes, she is also God?' (p. 371). And this is a

logical conundrum she cannot escape. She can state, compellingly, the values to which a novelist must remain loyal; but whether the fiction she constructs will constitute adequate atonement for the original crime is, perhaps, up to the reader to judge. 'The attempt was all' (p. 371), she concludes.

McEwan, speaking through Robbie, comments on the difficulties of establishing the truth about historical events, especially in wartime (p. 227), throwing interesting light upon the role of the novelist. Robbie/McEwan says:

> Who could ever describe this confusion, and come up with the village names and the dates for the history books? And take the reasonable view and begin to assign the blame? No one would ever know what it was like to be here. Without the details there could be no larger picture. (p. 227)

From one point of view, what the novelist is doing is the work of the historian, recording the testimony of the characters who were there, and arguably presenting it to a wider public than a historian could (how many readers of *Atonement* have ever read a historical account of the withdrawal to Dunkirk?). Equally, though, unless the historian was there, no one can know whether the novelist's reconstruction is accurate or not. Once again, as Briony later says, the power of the novelist is comparable to that of God (p. 371) and cannot be held accountable. We happen to know that McEwan was particularly keen to reconstruct the withdrawal to Dunkirk because his own father was involved in it, and several details in the fictional account were in fact witnessed by McEwan senior. But we only know this because McEwan has told us so. If we are able to trust the novelist, then the reader is able to gain a picture of the events that is both historically and emotionally accurate.

Literary terms and concepts

Assessment Objective 1 requires 'insight appropriate to literary study, using appropriate terminology' and therefore a knowledge of literary terms is a necessity for A-level English literature students. It has the further benefit of allowing responses to text to be precise and concise. The literary terms below, many of which will already be known from GCSE studies, are used in this book and are relevant to an understanding of the traditions and styles of the novel. You may wish to add examples from the text next to the relevant definitions.

cliché	a predictable and overused expression or situation
closure	a sense of an ending, tying up the ends in a fictional work
contextuality	the historical, social and cultural background of a text
epigraph	an inscription at the head of a book or chapter

epistolary	taking the form of letters
eponymous	a literary work whose title is the name of a central character, e.g. *Clarissa*
faction	the mixing of historical and fictional characters and events in one work
genre	type or form of writing
intertextuality	relationship between one text and another
irony	language intended to mean the opposite of the words actually expressed; or an amusing or cruel reversal of a situation that is expected, intended or deserved
metafiction	a work of fiction that self-consciously addresses the devices of fiction
monologue	an extended speech or thought process by one character; it is dramatic monologue if other characters are present and actions are being performed at the same time
persona	a voice within a text that plays the role of narrator
plurality	possible multiple meanings of a text
Postmodernism	a contemporary literary movement, beginning around 1950 (see section on 'Postmodernism' in 'Literary context' on pp. 26–28)
prolepsis	an anticipation of future events
romance	a popular story of love and war, deriving from medieval court life and fairy tale
self-reflexive	term describing a work that calls explicit attention to how it has been constructed
stereotype	a category of person with typical characteristics (e.g. a British army officer), often used for mockery

Questions & Answers

Essay questions, specimen plans and examiner notes

Exam essays

Refer to pp. 5–13 for a more detailed discussion of examination essay techniques. You may be studying *Atonement* for an open- or a closed-book examination, but in either case you need to know exactly which Assessment Objectives are being tested by your exam board and where the heaviest weighting falls. You will probably have looked at or practised past-paper questions so that you know what kind of title to expect, and it would be helpful if your teacher shared with you the examiners' reports for previous years' exams. Close reference to text is required even in closed-text exams, and as quotation demonstrates 'use of text' it is often the most concise way of supporting a point. You are, however, more likely in a closed-text exam to be set a general question dealing with structural or generic issues, theme or characterisation, often based on a critical comment. Even in an open-book exam the best-performing students do not need to refer to their text very often, so do not be intimidated if you are sitting a closed-book exam.

Essay questions fall into the following categories: close section analysis and relation to whole text; characterisation; setting and atmosphere; sequence and structure; genre; language and style; themes and issues. Remember, however, that themes are relevant to all essays, and that analysis, not just description, is always required. Exam essays should be clearly structured, briskly argued, concisely expressed, closely focused, and supported by brief but constant textual references. They should show a combination of familiarity, understanding, analytical skill and informed personal response. Length is not in itself an issue — quality matters rather than quantity — but you have to prove your knowledge and fulfil the assessment criteria, and without sufficient coverage and exploration of the title you cannot be awarded a top mark. Aim realistically for approximately 12 paragraphs or four sides of A4.

Do not take up one absolute position and argue only one interpretation. There are no 'yes' or 'no' answers in literature. The other side must have something to be said for it or the question would not have been set, so consider both views before deciding which one to argue, and mention the other one first to prove your awareness of different reader opinions. It is permissible to say your response is equally balanced, provided that you have explained the contradictory evidence and have proved that ambivalence is built into the text.

Exam essay process

The secret of exam essay success is a good plan, which gives coverage and exploration of the title and refers to the four elements of text: plot, characterisation, language and themes. Think about the issues freshly rather than attempt to regurgitate your own or someone else's ideas, and avoid giving the impression of a pre-packaged essay you are determined to deliver whatever the title.

When you've chosen a question, underline its key words and define them briefly, in as many ways as are relevant to the text, to form the introduction and provide the background. Plan the rest of the essay, staying focused on the question, in approximately 12 points, recorded as short phrases and with indications of evidence. Include a concluding point which does not repeat anything already said but which pulls your ideas together to form an overview. It may refer to other readers' opinions, refer back to the title, or include a relevant quotation from the text or elsewhere.

Check your plan to see that you have dealt with all parts of the question, have used examples of the four elements of text in your support, and have analysed, not just described. Remind yourself of the Assessment Objectives (printed on the exam paper). Group points and organise the plan into a structure with numbers, brackets or arrows.

Tick off the points in your plan as you use them in writing your essay, and put a diagonal line through the whole plan once you have finished. You can add extra material as you write, as long as it does not take you away from the outline you have constructed.

Concentrate on expressing yourself clearly as you write your essay, and on writing accurately, concisely and precisely (e.g. 'the long vowel sounds create a mournful effect' is more specific than 'it sounds sad'). Integrate short quotations throughout the essay.

Allow five minutes at the end for checking and improving your essay in content and style. Insertions and crossings-out, if legible, are encouraged. As well as checking accuracy of spelling, grammar and punctuation, watch out for errors of fact, name or title slips, repetition, and absence of linkage between paragraphs. Make sure your conclusion sounds conclusive, and not as though you have run out of time, ink or ideas. A few minutes spent checking can make the difference of a grade.

Planning practice

It is a useful activity to play at being examiners and to try thinking of essay titles for planning practice. This makes you think about the main issues, some perhaps

not previously considered, and which episodes would lend themselves as support for whole-text questions. Try to use the kind of language examiners use for expressing titles, which must avoid vagueness and ambiguity.

Using some of the titles below, practise planning essay titles within a time limit of 8 minutes, using about half a page. Aim for at least ten points and know how you would support them. Use numbers to structure the plan. Do this in groups and exchange and compare plans. Get used to using note form and abbreviations for names to save time, and to either not using your text (for closed-book examinations) or using it as little as possible.

Since beginnings are the most daunting part of the essay for many students, you could also practise opening paragraphs for your planned essays. Remember to define the terms of the title, especially any abstract words, and this will give your essay breadth, depth and structure. For instance, if the word 'wartime' appears, say exactly what you take 'wartime' to mean, and how it applies to the novel you have studied.

Students also find conclusions difficult, so experiment with final paragraphs for the essays you have planned. The whole essay is working towards the conclusion, so you need to know what it is going to be before you start writing the essay, and to make it clear that you have proved your case.

Exam questions

OCR English Literature A2 Unit 2712

This is an open-book examination. Candidates are required to answer one Section A question and one Section B question, which may be on the same book.

Section A

1 By careful comparison of two passages from *Atonement*, explore the presentation of the character of Cecilia.

2 By careful comparison of two passages from *Atonement*, investigate the portrayal of the effects of the Second World War on two different characters.

3 By careful consideration of two passages from *Atonement*, discuss the importance of place in the novel.

4 Compare and contrast the attitudes to Robbie Turner of two characters in *Atonement* as presented in Part One of the novel.

5 Compare and contrast the presentation of two of the characters in Part One of *Atonement*.

6 By careful comparison of two passages from *Atonement*, explore the presentation of social class.

Section B

1 Do you consider *Atonement* to be a war novel, or merely a novel set in wartime?

2 How important is social class in determining the events in *Atonement*?

3 The narrative of *Atonement* is presented from a number of perspectives, but it transpires that all are in fact written by Briony Tallis. How successfully does she vary the style of her writing to disguise this fact?

4 Briony claims to have achieved 'an impartial psychological realism' (p. 41) in her writing. Is this borne out by the first three parts of *Atonement*?

5 '*Atonement* is a novel about the business of writing novels.' Do you agree with this assessment?

6 'Above all, the reader is angry at being deceived by the first three parts.' Is this your view of *Atonement*?

7 'A silly, hysterical little girl.' Is this description by Cecilia a fair assessment of Briony at the time, and does it reduce the culpability of her actions?

8 Who do you consider is principally responsible for the unjust imprisonment of Robbie Turner?

9 'The reader of *Atonement* is angered by McEwan's failure to include key episodes in the novel.' Do you agree with this judgement?

10 Do any of the characters in the novel succeed in atoning for their sins?

Edexcel English Literature A2 Unit 6

This is a closed-book, comparative-text examination, on the theme 'Divided Societies'. *Atonement* is to be compared with *North and South* by Elizabeth Gaskell. (It is recommended that candidates answer some of the general questions above in order to secure their knowledge and understanding of the text prior to attempting the comparative questions below.)

1 'Some may think, but most must labour.' Compare and contrast your two novels in such a way as to explore in some detail this view of the influence of commercialism in them.

2 'Author and characters rarely speak with the same voice and, like the characters, the reader must lay aside prejudice and assumption and be willing to learn.' Compare and contrast your two novels in such a way as to explore in some detail the extent to which you agree with this critical statement.

3 'The presentation of division in such novels as these depends as much on social environment as on personal relationships.' Discuss how far you find this view acceptable by comparing and contrasting the two novels you have studied for this paper.

4 'However much modern critics may argue to the contrary, the final message of all "socially aware" novels such as these is that the individual is always more

important than the group.' By comparing and contrasting the two novels you have prepared for this paper discuss how far you find this an acceptable judgement.

Examiner notes, specimen plans and mark schemes

OCR English Literature A2 Unit 2712: Section A

1 By careful comparison of two passages from *Atonement*, explore the presentation of the character of Cecilia.

OCR mark scheme

Notes on the task. Through their selection and comparison of appropriate passages candidates address AO2ii. Their close study of the passages (AO3) must focus on the author's presentation of Cecilia and must address the concept of 'character'.

Top band descriptor. *Answers that are penetrating and original* and which should:

- show assured presentation of cogent arguments, using appropriate terminology (AO1)
- contain sophisticated understanding of *Atonement* as a novel encompassing a range of elements, exploring and commenting in depth on similarities and differences in McEwan's presentation of Cecilia in two passages, and making accurate and relevant cross-reference to other passages (noting the variety of presentation of Cecilia in the novel, and contrasting the presentation in Part One and Part Three) (AO2ii)
- demonstrate insight into how McEwan exploits form and language (overall structure, internal monologues, dialogue, vocabulary, for instance) to present Cecilia in different lights and to different effect (AO3)

2 By careful comparison of two passages from *Atonement*, investigate the portrayal of the effects of the Second World War on two different characters.

Possible plan

- Select two characters: Robbie and Briony.
- Select passages: e.g. Robbie p. 263; Briony p. 292.
- Directly compare passages. Each is a reflective internal monologue by the character concerned.
- Both are shocked and sickened by what they have witnessed (Robbie along the route of defeat, Briony in the hospital).
- Both reflect upon their failure to do more, e.g. Briony: 'The moment the war touched her life, at the first moment of pressure, she had failed' (p. 292). Robbie: 'But first he must cover the miles again…and ask the Flemish lady and her son if they held him accountable for their deaths' (p. 263).

- Both are in an extreme physical condition at the time: Briony is exhausted and shocked from helping the first batch of wounded soldiers; Robbie is ill and partly delirious, but he has been feeling guilt all the way along the road. Compare language of two extracts.
- Both have been helpless witnesses to atrocities that they are not responsible for.
- Both have done their best to help, so far as it lay in their power, e.g. Briony patiently nursed the dying French soldier, Robbie attempted to rescue the Flemish woman and her child.
- Despite the possible dehumanising effects of what they have witnessed, both retain their humanity; e.g. Robbie helps rescue the RAF man from the mindless attack by other soldiers; Briony is shocked at her own limitations but finds reserves of strength to carry on.
- The experience of war hardens the determination of each to do what they have resolved to do: Robbie to survive and get back to Cecilia (although he fails to do so); Briony to endure the humiliation of withdrawing her statement in order to make restitution to Robbie and Cecilia (which she also fails to do).
- Possible comparison with other characters: while others are suffering, Marshall and Lola get rich out of making chocolate and get married, without any apparent consideration for those who have suffered for Marshall's unpunished crime. This reinforces the bleak view that there is no justice, especially in wartime.
- Conclusion: war places people in extreme situations and makes unreasonable demands upon them. Both characters show their humanity by feeling guilt at their failure to do the impossible, and by feeling compassion for the victims.

OCR English Literature A2 Unit 2712: Section B

1 Do you consider *Atonement* to be a war novel, or merely a novel set in wartime?

OCR mark scheme

Notes on the task. Candidates must produce an independent judgement based on their detailed reading of the novel (AO4). They also need to evaluate the different contextual influences that may affect their response to the question whether the book is a war novel (AO5ii).

Top band descriptor. *Answers that are penetrating and original* and which should:

- show assured presentation of cogent arguments, using appropriate terminology (AO1)
- demonstrate an individual and carefully considered judgement on the question of whether *Atonement* is in essence a war novel or a novel set in wartime, discriminating clearly between these two ideas (AO4)
- show a real appreciation of the influence of historical perspectives on their reading of the novel, as well as an appreciation of other perspectives (gender, political, social, cultural) (AO5ii)

2 How important is social class in determining the events in *Atonement*?

Possible plan

- Social class sets the background and lays the foundations for the tragedy.
- 'Natural' development of relationship between Robbie and Cecilia are hampered by awareness of class differences, especially at Cambridge, where Robbie can only study as the recipient of charity from Jack Tallis.
- Cecilia misunderstands the episode of Robbie removing his shoes, which sets the tone for subsequent misunderstanding of his motives and actions.
- Following the rape, class prejudice makes Tallises, police and courts believe Briony's uncorroborated story because rape was considered 'working-class' behaviour.
- This is reinforced by even Robbie and Cecilia assuming the real rapist must be Danny, again for class reasons, because they cannot imagine that upper-middle-class Marshall could be capable of such a thing. They are blinded by prejudiced assumptions and ignore key evidence of the struggle between Lola and Marshall earlier.
- All members of Tallis family are equally guilty, e.g. 'Now that I've broken away, I'm beginning to understand the snobbery that lay behind their stupidity. My mother never forgave you your first' (p. 209).
- It can also be argued that Jack's attitude to Robbie is a patronising and condescending form of charity; Emily dismisses it as a 'hobby', undertaken more to salve Jack's conscience than from any real compassion for Robbie.
- However, Briony's attitude to Robbie is more complex; she never explicitly shows class prejudice towards him. Her attitude may be coloured by her earlier feelings towards him (related by Robbie on pp. 229–32).
- Briefly point out the role of class in other events of the novel; e.g. Cecilia and Briony both become nurses to do their duty in time of war; Robbie witnesses class differences during the withdrawal to Dunkirk.
- Conclusion: class prejudice and assumptions underlie the whole of the central plot of the novel, and the novel can be viewed as an extended critique of a set of assumptions that is so unthinkingly accepted by all the middle-class characters and that blinds them to evidence and allows them to condemn an innocent man.

Edexcel English Literature A2 Unit 6

1 'Some may think, but most must labour.' Compare and contrast your two novels in such a way as to explore in some detail this view of the influence of commercialism in them.

Edexcel mark scheme

AO2ii   It is to be hoped that candidates think about the implications of the epigrammatic proposition at the heart of this question before embarking on their answers. Lower band answers will most likely use the polarities of thinking and doing as

a way of exploring the masters and men divide that these candidates prepare so thoroughly. Higher band answers are likely to be more aware of the way in which the task develops the quotation by mentioning 'the influence of commercialism' and structure their material accordingly.

AO4   This question is more contentious than it may at first appear in some particularly lower band answers which may rely on stereotyping the social divide. Higher band answers may well adopt a line whereby they argue that while few thinkers actually labour in these novels – with the possible exception of *Atonement* – there are plenty of examples – not just Stephen Blackpool – of labourers and toilers who think.

AO5ii   Social division is, of course, at the heart of this question, which provides even lower band answers with plenty of opportunities to demonstrate their knowledge and understanding of their novels' socio-historical context. Higher band answers will no doubt explore this material too but less as an end in itself and more as a means of exploring the parallel similarities and differences in their chosen texts.

2   'Author and characters rarely speak with the same voice and, like the characters, the reader must lay aside prejudice and assumption and be willing to learn.' Compare and contrast your two novels in such a way as to explore in some detail the extent to which you agree with this critical statement.

Edexcel mark scheme

AO2ii   The question is not just about narrative method but about the experience of being a reader, though lower band answers may only show awareness of the former. Higher band answers may well find that their own reading experience and the insights gained from studying the two novels they have put together for this question are paralleled by the experiences of certain carefully selected characters, though they also need to establish links between the two texts, not just within them separately.

AO4   Whether or not candidates agree with the proposition here, there needs to be some appreciation that narrative method is a central concern of this question, though many lower band answers may simply assert and assume that authors do use their central characters to voice their own views. Higher band answers are more likely to use exploration and analysis of relevant text to assess or evaluate this part of the proposition before seeking parallels between reader and character instead of just focusing exclusively on writer and character.

AO5ii   The notions of prejudice and assumption voiced in the question are there to give access to the context of personal reading as well as the social and moral contexts of the novels. Lower band answers may rather skirt round the issues

here or at best define them somewhat loosely whereas higher band answers will be more likely to explore parallels both between the reader/writer and character relationship and the experiences encountered by these same characters which become a part of the reader's own experience. A-level candidates cannot, of course, be expected to put things in these terms necessarily but there are some who will, just as we shall no doubt encounter some who put them rather better.

Sample essays

Below are two essays of different types, both falling within the top band. You can judge them against the Assessment Objectives for this text for your exam board and decide on the mark you think each deserves and why. You may be able to see ways in which each could be improved in terms of content, style and accuracy.

Sample essay 1: general question

How important is social class in determining the events in *Atonement*?

Social class plays a key role in *Atonement*; it establishes the background to the events and lays the foundations for the tragedy. A series of misunderstandings and misinterpretations set in train the events that culminate in Robbie Turner being wrongfully imprisoned for a crime that he did not commit; prejudices and assumptions based on class stereotypes contribute to this process at several points. Most importantly, though, his conviction on the flimsiest of evidence reveals how pervasive attitudes to class were in England in the 1930s.

Robbie Turner and Cecilia Tallis were the same age, shared a love of English literature and grew up together in the idyllic surroundings of the Tallis house in Surrey. Although separated at school (Robbie went to the local grammar school, while Cecilia was sent away to board at Roedean) they went up to Cambridge together, albeit to separate colleges (there being no mixed colleges at Cambridge until 40 years later). But they were separated by a much more fundamental divide: Cecilia was the daughter of a wealthy, upper-middle-class senior civil servant, and Robbie was the son of the Tallises' cleaner. Even though they had grown up together, and Robbie 'had spent his childhood moving freely between the bungalow and the main house' (p. 86), this social gulf was unbridgeable. Arguably, it had been accentuated by their time at Cambridge, where they had moved in very different circles; she seems to have avoided him, and he had to adopt a robust response when asked about his humble origins.

Their potential relationship is further complicated by the fact that not only is Robbie the child of the Tallises' servant, and in the 1930s such a relaxed attitude to social inferiors was not unknown, but that he was the recipient of Jack Tallis's charitable patronage. It was Jack's money that enabled him to go to Cambridge, and Emily Tallis, Cecilia's mother, resented it, viewing him as 'a hobby of Jack's' (p. 151). All of these factors combine to prevent the emergence of a natural relationship between these two who have known each

other for so long, share so much and are both otherwise devoid of special friends at the age of 23.

It is against this class background that the events of Part One of the novel must be seen. The mixture of irritation, showing off and contempt, which underlie Cecilia's stripping to her underwear to retrieve the pieces from the broken Meissen vase, reveal the complexity of the emotions in play that day. Many factors have contributed to it: Cecilia has spent the summer after coming down from Cambridge with her family, but she has achieved nothing; Robbie is going on to study for a medical degree, which Cecilia views as another in a succession of his 'fads', but one which will cost the family dear to support him. The recent incident in which Robbie removed his shoes on entering the house was explicitly misinterpreted by Cecilia as an insult. The breaking of the vase itself (a symbol of the wealth of the Tallises) is the consequence of misunderstanding; he wants to help her but does not understand what she is trying to do. Her undressing is designed to prevent him from atoning for breaking the vase by rescuing the pieces, although he interprets it as deliberate 'humiliation' (p. 80). Subconsciously, of course, there may have been more going on, which not even Cecilia was aware of; angry though he was, Robbie registered 'her breasts wide apart and small' (p. 79) as well as 'the triangular darkness her knickers were supposed to conceal' (p. 79), but interprets this not as sexual display but as treating him 'as though he were an infant' (p. 80).

Social class, though, is not responsible for all the misunderstandings that contributed to the day's outcome. Briony, also observing Cecilia in the fountain, sees it very differently, helping to establish the frame of mind in which her later interception of Robbie's sexually explicit letter to Cecilia allows her to view him as a 'maniac' (the word suggested by Lola). When she sees Cecilia and Robbie making love in the library, she assumes that he is assaulting her because she cannot imagine it any differently. Nevertheless, none of these things lead to Robbie being imprisoned. They do, however, explain how it was that Briony was able to persuade herself that the rapist must have been Robbie, even though she could not clearly identify the fleeing figure when she came upon Lola on the slope by the Greek temple.

Lola's contribution to Robbie's conviction is important. She has ample opportunity to correct what she must quickly realise to be Briony's misidentification; although we are not given any insight into her thought processes, it is likely that she went along with Briony's suggestions not only as a way of avoiding blame for complicity in what had happened, but because she could see that Robbie would make a plausible candidate for the role of rapist (she and Briony had, after all, discussed him as a 'maniac' just a few hours previously).

More shocking is the fact that Cecilia's mother, brother, father, the police and the courts were all willing to believe Briony's uncorroborated story about a Cambridge graduate, with an unblemished record, whom all but the police had known personally since he was a boy, because rape was considered a 'working-class' behaviour. This is powerful testament to the power of class prejudice – albeit undoubtedly helped by a dose of puritanical shock at the explicit nature of Robbie's letter to Cecilia, which Briony had helpfully given to the police.

What is even more revealing is that Robbie and Cecilia, who know perfectly well that Robbie was not the rapist, assume that it must have been the working-class Danny Hardman (the only other male not accounted for) because it was unthinkable that the upper-middle-class millionaire Marshall could be capable of such a thing. They, like the others, are so blinded by prejudiced assumptions that they ignore key evidence of the struggle between Lola and Marshall earlier (the scratches on Lola and Marshall, and the cry from the playroom heard by Emily). When Briony is able to tell them what really happened (which she has only pieced together by seeing Marshall and Lola at their wedding), a further overlooked piece of evidence is recalled: Marshall and Robbie are the same height, whereas Danny was not. Briony could not possibly have mistaken Danny for Robbie, and yet prejudice had persuaded Cecilia and Robbie that it must be so.

Hindsight lends added perspective. Looking back in 1940, Cecilia writes to Robbie: 'Now that I've broken away, I'm beginning to understand the snobbery that lay behind their stupidity. My mother never forgave you your first' (p. 209). Emily's resentment at Jack's patronising and condescending charity towards Robbie may also have played a part.

At this point it should be recalled that all of Part One is told, in retrospect, by Briony, who was no doubt attempting to reconstruct the attitudes of most of those involved, even if she is not attempting to minimise her own guilt. Equally, because we are not presented with any of the events following Robbie's arrest, the reader can only speculate on what must have taken place; but Cecilia's revelation that she loved Robbie (which we presume she must have made) may have fed prejudiced feelings that Robbie was not a suitable partner for Cecilia and that prison would keep him out of the way. Briony's own feelings towards Robbie may have been complex, as she hints by twice telling (with very different emphases) the story of how she had been childishly in love with Robbie three summers previously and had tested his loyalty to her. There is a suspicion that Briony may have harboured some jealousy at Robbie falling for Cecilia rather than her. However it is looked at, there were a range of reasons why various characters were happy for Robbie to be convicted for this crime, some knowing and others perhaps merely suspecting that this may not have been the entire truth about the events of that fateful June evening.

Social class plays a role in other parts of the novel too. In Part Two, the two working-class corporals who accompany Robbie in the retreat to Dunkirk note his natural leadership potential, although he is of lower rank than them, and all three are portrayed as more admirable than the supposedly socially superior officers. Both Cecilia and Briony volunteer for the lower-class occupation of nursing in order to make their contribution to the war effort, and witness a similar breakdown of traditional class roles to that witnessed by Robbie in France.

It is clear that class-based prejudices and attitudes underlie the whole of the central plot of the novel, which can be viewed as an extended critique of a set of assumptions so unthinkingly accepted by all the middle-class characters that it blinds them to important evidence and allows them to condemn an innocent man.

Sample essay 2: extract-based question

By careful comparison of two passages from *Atonement*, investigate the portrayal of the effects of the Second World War on two different characters.

As is frequently the case with novels set during the Second World War, the advent of war brings both new pressures and new opportunities for the characters. In the case of *Atonement*, the events of the preceding years of peace have themselves been severely traumatic for the central characters and, unusually, war offers all of them a fresh start. For Robbie Turner, falsely imprisoned for the rape of under-age Lola Quincey on the basis of the biased testimony of 13-year-old Briony Tallis, war brings the chance to substitute military service for prison. For Briony Tallis, now five years older and painfully aware of the injustice she has done, war offers her the chance to make atonement for her crime.

Robbie Turner provides the voice and perspective for the whole of Part Two of the novel, when he, with two corporals, is making his way to Dunkirk following the catastrophic collapse of the British Expeditionary Force in Belgium in May 1940. In a passage on pp. 262–63, having finally arrived at Bray-les-Dunes and awaiting evacuation, but deliriously ill, he looks back at key incidents on the way. Although Robbie has been the entirely innocent victim of an appalling miscarriage of justice, he is plagued by his conscience, especially about two incidents where, he feels, he should have done more, although neither was his responsibility in any sense. Part Two begins with the horror of seeing a boy's severed leg in a tree (p. 192); retracing his steps in his mind to that point, Robbie wishes that he could 'Gather up from the mud the pieces of burned, striped cloth, the shreds of his pyjamas, then bring him down, the poor pale boy, and make a decent burial. A nice-looking kid. Let the guilty bury the innocent, and let no one change the evidence' (pp. 262–63). Robbie feels the need to atone for a crime that someone else committed, and the phrase 'let no one change the evidence' shows that he is conflating this with his own false conviction.

The second incident is one in which he is even more blameless, when he helped a Flemish mother and her young child to flee from an attacking German Stuka dive bomber. In his delirium, he feels he must 'cover the miles again…and ask the Flemish lady and her son if they held him accountable for their deaths.' This is an extraordinary reversal of what happened: he helped the mother and child away from the road, but they then refused to move further to safety, even though he implored them too. They were killed by the next bomb. Robbie's sense of guilt tortures him, even though the responsibility is in no way his. He is reminded again of the events of June 1935 leading up to his imprisonment: 'You carried the twins, but not us, no.' It is one of the great ironies of the novel that Robbie spent all night dutifully searching for the Quincey twins, finding them and bringing them back safely the following morning, only to find, to his bewilderment, that he was under arrest for someone else's crime.

Briony Tallis provides the voice and perspective for the whole of Part Three of the novel. She has voluntarily renounced her coveted place at Girton College, Cambridge, in order to become a nurse. Her elder sister Cecilia, also a nurse, comments 'I get the

impression she's taken on nursing as a sort of penance' (p. 212). Along with many other middle-class girls who have volunteered to make their contribution to the war effort in this way, Briony finds the discipline harsh and the duties demeaning, but she is so convinced of her own guilt and unworthiness that she accepts them uncomplainingly. When, however, war casualties finally arrive, after a long period of preparation, she finds herself sorely tested, and in a passage on p. 292 she reflects on her own inadequacy: 'The moment the war touched her life, at the first moment of pressure, she had failed.' But, despite her guilt, the failure was actually merely physical; she was not strong enough to carry a loaded stretcher very far. She displays moral courage in dealing with the appallingly wounded soldiers thereafter.

Each of these passages is a reflective internal monologue by the character, in a time of pressure and stress, and each feels that they have failed. By their own standards, they have failed tests that they have set themselves. This is a very important moral dimension of the novel: in the midst of the inhumanity and atrocities of war, each retains their own humanity, decency and set of values. This is perhaps more impressive for Robbie, who has strong grounds for resentment anyway, and who has been through an extended experience that has dehumanised many of those around him. But for Briony too, headstrong, selfish and spoiled as she clearly was as a young girl (the youngest, indulged daughter of a mother who sought to delay the growing up of her final child), this marks a significant moral development. Although her reaction to her perceived failure is to give up ('If she dropped her end she would simply leave, gather her things from her room into her suitcase, and go to Scotland and work as a land-girl. It would be better for everyone') she does not in fact do so, but finds the reserves to carry on and do her duty.

Both of these characters are significantly changed from when the reader last encountered them in Part One of the novel. But in both cases, because of the great narrative gap between 1935 and 1940, it is hard to evaluate the role of war in these changes. Robbie has grown up, become more single-minded and determined (he used to drive Cecilia wild because of the 'fads' he flitted between), and has developed clear leadership skills (the corporals, Nettle and Mace, defer to him, despite his inferior rank, because 'He acted like an officer, but he didn't even have a single stripe', p. 193). We do not know, however, whether this is a result of his experiences in prison, the realisation that Cecilia has remained faithful to him, or his harrowing experiences in Belgium and France. Similarly, although Briony in 1940 is very different from what she herself, looking back 64 years later, describes as 'that busy, priggish, conceited little girl' (p. 367), the mere fact of ageing from 13 to 18 might be enough to account for such a transformation, let alone the shocking realisation of the enormity of the crime she has committed by falsely incriminating Robbie for a crime of which he was wholly innocent. The war has offered her an opportunity to make atonement in a more general way, but she is determined to do so directly as well by recanting her false evidence. The war has probably had little to do with this determination, although the reader is frustrated that McEwan gives no indication at all of the process by which Briony came to realise the truth about what she had done.

There are significant parallels between the two characters in the two chosen passages. Both are in an extreme physical condition at the time: Briony is exhausted and shocked from helping the first batch of wounded soldiers; Robbie is ill and partly delirious, but he has been feeling guilt all the way along the road. Both have been shocked and sickened as helpless witnesses to atrocities for which they are not responsible. Both have done their best to help, so far as it lay in their power; Briony later patiently nursed the dying French soldier, and Robbie attempted to rescue the Flemish woman and her child. Most importantly, despite the possible dehumanising effects of what they have witnessed, both retain their humanity: Robbie helps rescue the RAF man from the mindless attack by other soldiers; Briony is shocked at her own limitations but finds reserves of strength to carry on. The experience of war hardens the determination of each to do what they have resolved to do: Robbie to survive and get back to Cecilia (although he fails to do so, through no fault of his own); Briony to endure the humiliation of withdrawing her statement in order to make restitution to Robbie and Cecilia (which she also fails to do, also through no fault of hers). The language of the passages reflects their mental state in each case. For Robbie, his delirium leads to the breakdown of his grammar: 'You carried the twins, but not us, no. No, you are not guilty. No.' This repetition is typical of a fatigued, delirious mental state. Briony's language remains more literary and considered, even in this moment of stress, but her sentences are uncharacteristically short and blunt, and the repetition of 'if' reinforces her confusion and uncertainty in the face of her perceived failure.

It is noteworthy that while both Robbie and Briony find that their strength of character remains undiminished by the experience of war, other characters respond very differently. In particular, Paul Marshall and Lola Quincey, the two people equally responsible for Robbie's false imprisonment because both know what really happened that June evening, get rich out of making chocolate and get married, while others are suffering, without any apparent consideration for those who have suffered for Marshall's unpunished crime. This reinforces the bleak view that there is no justice, especially in wartime. The subsequent fates of Robbie and Cecilia, both killed by the war before the end of 1940, are a further indication of this.

In conclusion, it is fair to say that war places people in extreme situations and makes unreasonable demands upon them. Both Robbie and Briony show their humanity by feeling guilt at their failure to do the impossible, and by feeling compassion for the victims. Both have found reserves of character in the extreme situations in which they find themselves, although it is impossible to say how far this might have happened in more ordinary circumstances had they not become caught up in the Second World War.

Further study

There are many books about Britain during the Second World War. The most recent is *Wartime: Britain 1939–1945* by Juliet Gardiner (2004, paperback 2005), a highly readable account based principally upon personal testimony. For the evacuation of Dunkirk in Operation 'Dynamo', see **en.wikipedia.org/wiki/ Dunkirk_evacuation**.

No books of criticism have yet been published on *Atonement*; this is not uncommon for modern fiction, and the bulk of the critical responses available are in the form of reviews of the novel.

An excellent extended critique of *Atonement* by Brian Finney of California State University, Long Beach, may be found at **www.csulb.edu/~bhfinney/McEwan.html**.

www.complete-review.com/reviews/mcewani/atonement.htm is an index of all available reviews of the novel.

Other useful links may be found at **www.authortrek.com/atonement_page.html** and **www.authortrek.com/ian_mcewan_page.html**.

Ian McEwan's official website may be found at **www.ianmcewan.com/**. It has an exhaustive list of reviews of, and articles on, the novel, at **www.ianmcewan.com /bib/books/atonement.html**.

There is an interesting series of four articles by John Mullan, originally published in the *Guardian*, which are at:
http://books.guardian.co.uk/review/story/0,12084,908978,00.html
http://books.guardian.co.uk/review/story/0,12084,913661,00.html
http://books.guardian.co.uk/reviewbookclub/story/0,12286,918616,00.html
http://books.guardian.co.uk/review/story/0,12084,923904,00.html

For Elizabeth Bowen, see **www.usna.edu/EnglishDept/ilv/bowen.htm**.

Film version

A film version of *Atonement* is in prospect, and filming started in June 2006 with release scheduled for August 2007. It has been adapted from the novel by the playwright Christopher Hampton, and is directed by Joe Wright, with Keira Knightley playing Cecilia, James McAvoy playing Robbie and Saoirse Ronan playing Briony; details (regularly updated) are available at **www.hollywood.com/movies/ detail/id/3464413**.